Betty-Anne's

HELPFUL HOUSEHOLD HINTS

VOLUME I

Betty-Anne Hastings
with Mary-Beth Connors

VENTURA BOOKS
New York City
Printed in the United States

Ventura Associates, Inc.
200 Madison Avenue/New York, 10016

INTRODUCTION

Our economy, and the changing, sometimes frightening world we live in, doesn't seem to be getting any better. As prices go up, though, it often seems that quality goes down, and not only does the money not go as far, but nothing lasts as long! Times like these need a helpful hand, and a little ingenuity would help, too.

I've endeavored to fill this book with helpful hints, timely tips, and money-saving ideas. For instance, I've catalogued a number of hints for pets, everything from cleaning cat-hairs off your furniture quickly, to a tip on getting your dog to take his medicine, and like it, too. You'll find tips for vacation-time, ideas to keep your kids amused on rainy days, a bevy of recycling "tricks" to get added life out of things you might have thrown away, not to mention the load of special care hints for your extra-special clothes, or the huge group of household tips I've gathered from friends, relatives, and acquaintances.

I've divided this book into easy-to-read sections, with like hints assembled in chapters. Many of my friends tell me that they keep a volume handy wherever they are working, in the kitchen, laundry, or bath for that necessary tip they may need, and to that end I've tried to make this book an easy-to-use "tool", one that will cut your work load and take a little of the burden off your over-burdened pocketbook.

Betty-Anne Hastings

Betty-Anne's Helpful Household Hints - Volume I

CONTENTS

1. **A Potpourri of More Household Hints**
   We've assembled a collection that includes tips for lightening your household chores, cleaning hints, some tips on repairing your favorite clothes, and even some that'll make your over-burdened budget look a little better.
2. **Recycling Tips and Helpers**
   Ever wondered what to do with those old newspapers that have been cluttering the garage for so long? Or how to put to good use those old nylon net vegetable bags? Or even the excess hair you clean out of your brushes and combs? Well, we give you the answers to those questions and many more in our dazzling compendium of recycling tips.
3. **Gardening Victories**
   If you think your thumb will never be green, this chapter is for you. We've gathered some great tips on the care and feeding of your flowers and plants. Even if your thumb is purple, these things will give you a fighting chance.

4. **Clothing Care Tips**
   With the price of clothes today, we decided to reassemble a chapter on clothing care and maintenance, especially for you. Here are specific tips for your most delicate lingerie, and guidelines to keep your designer jeans looking great. We've even added a tip or two on sewing.
5. **Traveling and Vacation Hints**
   Vacations and traveling time should be peaceful, rest inducing, and above all, pleasant. We can't account for the weather, but we can help you enjoy yourself more with these fabulous tips.
6. **Our Furry Friends**
   Everyone loves their pets, but they don't always enjoy taking care of them. We've assembled some great tips, though, to make that more fun, and less time-consuming, too. To that end, why not take Rover out for a long walk and enjoy yourself?
7. **The Kids**
   Raising children has probably never been easy, but in these hectic times, you need all the help, and any tips, you can get. We've assembled some real beauties here, for children of all ages.

A POTPOURRI OF MORE HOUSEHOLD HINTS

In this incredibly helpful chapter, we've assembled what we consider to be the best of the best; each and every one of them a gem we wanted to share with you. You see, we know what it takes to maintain a modern household. Today's housewife and mother may also have a career to think about, too. According to recent statistics, an "ordinary" housewife spends an average of over 90 hours a week on maintaining and running a home! That's an enormous amount of time and energy expended. These hints and tips, however, were assembled with *you* in mind. We know they'll help you save time and money, rescue you from minor disasters and make life just a little easier (and less hectic!) all the way around.

Oven racks are just as hard to clean as your outdoor grill! But they don't have to be. Just apply a version of this little trick. Soak the racks in your bathtub. Just fill the tub with hot water, add dishwasher brand detergent (it's made for this sort of thing) and a little white vinegar to cut the grease. Put your feet up for an hour while that dirt and grime soaks away! Rinse and presto.

Scrubbing your blender can be time-consuming, not to mention frustrating. Instead, the next time you have to clean it, try this. Fill the blender about half-way with very hot water and a generous amount of dishwashing liquid. Before turning it on, throw in a couple of medium-sized ice cubes, to dislodge any insistent pieces of food.

You can even fix loose kitchen floor tiles yourself. If you have any loose vinyl tiles, here's a quick fix-it hint. Place a slightly damp cloth over the loose tile. Now set your iron on "hot" and "iron" the loose tile. Soon, the tile adhesive will soften. Simply remove the cloth, putting down a dry rag, and pile with heavy books for about 3 hours.

Ashtrays needn't be a cleaning problem. For all your ashtrays (except your glass or crystal ones) just coat the surface with your favorite furniture polish. The protective coating will allow burns and ash build-up to just rinse out.

Is your cutting board stained and ugly? Once more, common laundry bleach will do the trick. Just whip up a solution of a couple of teaspoons of liquid bleach in a dishpan full of warm water, and scrub away. Be sure and rinse the board several times with very hot water to alleviate all trace of the bleach. Your cutting board will look like new.

Bleach can remove stains from more than just laundry. Try some regular bleach on stains on your kitchen vinyl flooring. You'll be surprised how easily the bleach lifts out food stains you've been trying to scrub away for months.

Dresser drawers sticking? If your dresser

drawers tug back every time you pull on them, here's a helpful hint. Just rub a bar of ordinary hand soap across the runners, and they'll move smoothly.

Here's a quick hint that'll make using a saw easier. A little kerosene on the blade of your hand saw will act as a lubricant and minimize your huffing and puffing on tight cuts.

Is your bathtub discolored? It's probably hard water stains. What to do? Try covering the tub in paper towels, soaking them in full strength vinegar. After a couple of hours, remove the soaked towels, and presto! Your tub will look like new.

How's your shower head? Tiny mineral deposits can easily clog the head. Try boiling it once a month in a mild solution of white vinegar and water, and you'll always be assured of a great shower.

Ever wondered how to clean your filmy glass shower doors? Try wiping them clean with any furniture polish that has lemon oil. If the film is really heavy, use a steel wool pad soaked in dishwashing liquid to make that glass sparkle.

Do your tools get rusty? Chances are that you just don't use them enough. After cleaning them with a little steel wool, try coating them with a thin topping of petroleum jelly, and they'll never rust again.

Do your windows rattle? Most old window frames do. If yours rattle, here's a quick hint that'll stop all that racket. Just lightly glue ordinary foot "corn pads" to the frames, and your life will be a lot quieter.

Want a tip to make those screws screw in easier? Tired of struggling with screws that just don't want to screw in? Try pushing your screws into a bar of hand soap first, before inserting.

Throw rugs a mess? Well, here's a great hint. Between washings, spruce up your throw rugs by tossing them into the dryer, on a no-heat setting. The dirt will fly out of them, and you'll never beat another rug again.

Even your frost free freezer got dirty! Just because it doesn't ice up doesn't mean it doesn't get dirty or collect odors. But here's an easy way to clean it: Mix a 1/2 cup of isopropyl alcohol with a dishpan full of lukewarm water. The alcohol will loosen any icy matter and sponge away dirt and odors. But best of all, because alcohol evaporates rapidly, you don't have to dry!

A little instant coffee will work wonders on your furniture. Just make a thick paste of your favorite instant and a little water, and rub it into the nicks and scratches on your dark wood furniture. You'll be overjoyed at how new and beautiful those pieces will look.

Ever wonder how to keep your painted cement floors from peeling? Before you paint them (again), try this. Pour a bottle of white vinegar in a bucket and "paint" your floors with it first. After the vinegar dries, apply a coat of paint. This will work on most metal surfaces, too.

Try this when you paint your wrought-iron garden furniture. All those details will ruin your brush and take hours to finish. Instead, just dab the paint on with an old kitchen sponge.

Do your throw rugs bunch up? Try double-edged masking tape on the corners of the under-surface of your rugs. It won't harm your floor or your rugs, and will keep those throws in place.

Painting tips: Ever had the loose bristles of a paintbrush stick to the wall and ruin your paint job? Well, here's an easy solution. Just run an old hair comb through the brush before you use it. It'll rid the brush of stray "hairs" and assure a spotless paint job.

Wicker can be difficult to clean, but only if you let it be! Try spraying your favorite dusting or furniture polish onto an inexpensive paintbrush. It'll easily get those hard-to-reach dust specks and best of all, it'll take a lot less time!

Cleaning the oven is no fun! Let's face it, no one likes to clean the oven. But, we've come up with an easy and efficient method. Just sponge on a generous amount of household ammonia before you go to bed and close the oven door. The next morning, let the oven air out, and then wipe it clean with no fuss or mess.

Is your brick fireplace discolored? Usually, this discoloring is caused by smoke and soot and the heat of the fire literally "bakes" it on. How to clean it off? Simple! Just use a spray-on oven cleaner. Your bricks will be clean again in no time.

Aluminum lawn furniture is a snap to care for. Just coat the aluminum with paste wax, the kind you use on your car, at the beginning of every season. It won't pit or scar, and will keep on looking new longer.

Fingerprints can ruin even shining wood furniture. Here's a quick hint that'll keep those nasty prints from showing up. After waxing a wood surface, rub a little corn starch into the surface. It'll remove any excess wax and keep your surface from showing prints and smudges.

Storage drawers often smell musty. Try placing an old, shallow dish filled with baking soda at the rear of the drawer. The baking soda will absorb all those musty odors and keep your drawers smelling fresh. Baking soda will work in closets, too. It'll even keep your fridge smelling fresh.

Even your dishwasher gets dirty. Worse, it gets stained and unappealing, too. No one wants to put their family dishes in a dishwasher that looks dirty. And simply running the wash cycle won't get rid of that dinginess. What to do? Well, once more, simple powdered laundry bleach is the solution. Just use it instead of your dishwasher detergent in an empty machine. Not only will it clean away the dirt and stains, but it'll disinfect, too.

Has your refrigerator lost its shine? Ordinary washings and scrubbings *may* get it clean, but they'll leave the finish dull and lifeless. Here's a great hint: try washing it in a mild solution of vinegar and water. Apply it with an old, soft cotton rag, such as a discarded t-shirt. It'll cut the grease, and shine the surface.

Is your kitchen sink rust stained? If you have a steel sink, it's easy to gather rust stains. Scrubbing may not be the answer. Make a thick paste of baking soda and water, leaving it on the stains while you go shopping. When you return, buff the entire sink in the paste with a damp cloth, and then rinse. Your stains will be gone.

Is the top of your stove dull from cleaning and scrubbing? Sure, you want it to be clean, but scouring powders often leave your stove looking old and lusterless. Try a little liquid car polish and a damp cloth to brighten the enamel or metal. It'll also help the food and grease to come off more easily.

Polishing chrome can be easy. Just take a small sheet of aluminum foil. Turn the shiniest side out. Dampen the chrome with water and polish with the foil. As you "polish" the chrome with the tin-foil, it'll turn black. But your chrome will shine like it did when it was new.

Wondering how to clean wood shavings off your file or rasp? A little masking tape will work wonders. Just cover the length of the file, press, and pull off those shavings! It's as easy as one, two, three!

Here's a way to prevent lime deposits from building up in your humidifier. Just drop an old copper scouring pad into the water container.

Wondering how to clean your venetian blinds? Hang the blinds in the shower, turn on the water and let the shower do all of the work! No more hours of work or painful cuts, and best of all, you can even let them drip dry.

Are there cracks in your old wooden doors? Don't replace the door! Instead, your local hardware can supply you with plastic wood and colorings to match the stain on your doors. Just mix the color and the plastic wood, and apply smoothly with a clean putty knife. A little fine sandpaper will complete the job.

Is your wallpaper coming loose? If it's just loose in a few small areas, take heart. You can fix it yourself. A thin coating of ordinary rubber cement applied to both the back of the paper and the wall surface and your troubles will be over in no time.

Wondering how to find the studs in your wall when you are hanging pictures? Simple! Moving out from the corner, just tap lightly with your hammer. The wall will sound hollow between studs. Remember — most studs are placed 16 to 24 inches apart. Once you've found one, the rest are easy.

Measure this substitute for a yardstick. If you can never find your yardstick when you need it, try measuring with a length of string. It'll work just as well, and you can even keep it in your pocket.

Small holes in your kitchen linoleum can be

fixed. If you kept some of the scraps, just throw a corner into your blender. Make sure it's a small piece. Mix the dust with a little clear shellac or even white glue, and fill the hole with your mixture. The next day, you won't even be able to find it.

Do your locks stick? Almost nothing is more frustrating or aggravating than a lock that sticks. Here's a quick tip for your next lock emergency. Just dust a little talcum powder into the sticking lock to loosen it.

There's nothing worse than a dull razor blade! But you may not have to throw it away yet. Try sharpening it on the striking edge of an old match book cover.

Do you have small holes in your windows? If you have tiny holes in your window panes, and were considering replacing the whole piece of glass, think again. A little clear nail polish will seal the hole and will be almost invisible.

Wondering how to keep screws from coming loose? Well, just put a drop or two of clear nailpolish into the hole before you finish tightening the screw, and you'll never have to worry about that screw popping loose.

Is your toilet bowl stained and ugly? Scouring may be a waste of energy. Get rid of those unsightly water stains with regular laundry bleach. If stains are on the side of the bowl above water level, simply soak paper towels in the bleach and "plaster" them over the stain. Your bowl will be sparkling white in no time!

Don't let lint get you down when you're cleaning your glass-top tables. Just add a capful of any fabric softener to a bucket of warm, clear water. After you wash the glass, rinse them with this mixture, they'll be sparkling and lint-free. Extra tip: This solution will work on plexiglass, too.

Cleaning the fireplace can be a messy job. Particularly when you're cleaning out the ashes from the grate. Here's a tip that'll make that messy job much easier. Use a plant mister to dampen the ashes before you sweep them out, and it'll keep them from flying all over your room.

Cleaning the outdoor grill is as much fun as cleaning your oven. But here's a tip that'll make it easier. Just place the grill in a large plastic garbage can and cover it generously with industrial strength detergent. Fill the can with water, and let the grill soak overnight. Almost all the baked-on dirt will hose right off when you rinse it.

Here's how to keep ice cubes from sticking to each other. When you make a bunch of ice cubes for parties, do they stick together, leaving you with just one huge cube instead of the multitude of small ones you needed? Well, next time, just dump the cubes into a brown paper bag before sticking them into the freezer, and you're guaranteed not to get stuck with an "iceberg".

Keep your cakes "hole" free. After you've finished mixing the batter for your cake, just run a knife through the batter. It'll take out any air holes and make sure you're not embarrassed by any holes in the finished cake that could cause it to collapse.

Look out "gourmet" popcorn! Those "gourmet" popcorn ads always claim that one of their other advantages is that they get "all" the kernels to pop. Well, here's a little secret that'll get your less expensive brand to pop more kernels, too. Keep the kernels cold in your frig until just before you're ready to throw them into the hot oil. You eliminate almost all the unpopped kernels.

Everyone loves chicken soup . . . But, in this hectic, modern world, who has the time to make it the old fashioned way? What's more who has the time to clean up all the mess *during* the cooking. Well, you don't have to. We've got a tip that'll let you have your soup and eat it, too! And, with almost no clean-up! Just put your whole chicken, vegetables, herbs, spices, whatever, into a disposable cheesecloth bag. All the goodness will strain out through the porous fabric, and the messy "glop" will stay in, and be easily taken care of at clean-up time.

Keeping brass clean and shining can be a full-time job . . . but only if you let it! Here's a little secret. We coat our freshly polished brass with a little wood finishing oil, say, tung oil. It'll make the shine last 3 times as long.

Note: Don't fret about how to clean the oil back off your brass! A little paint thinner on a soft, cotton cloth wiped over the surface of the brass removes the oil. Afterwards, you're ready to polish it, oil it, and sit back for another couple of months.

Typewriter keys smudged and dirty? A little nail polish remover and an old toothbrush are the perfect cleaning duo to keep those keys tapping.

Hanging plants are an attractive plus to any room. However, if you're like us, you probably don't like the clunky chains, rope, or macrame necessary to hang those little green beauties. Well, we've got a solution. Nylon fishing line is strong enough to support even large plants and best of all, it's clear!

Lost contact lenses: Make the room as dark as possible, and then shine a flashlight over the floor. The lens will glow.

How to get kids (and some grown-ups) to take nasty tasting pills or liquid medicines: Suck on an ice cube to numb the tastebuds. Medicines will become practically tasteless.

Safety first! Try this when discarding dry cleaner plastic bags. Tie them in knots before you put in the garbage. Make sure small animals and children can't entangle themselves.

How to bathe small babies in large bathtubs: Place a plastic clothes basket in the tub. Water will be able to flow in and out of the basket and baby will feel more secure.

Do away with expensive commercial handwipes. Simply mix three caps of baby shampoo with a spray bottle full of water. It works just as well, and costs a lot less.

Going on a long trip with small infants? Instead of packing or stopping to buy fresh milk, simply pack dry milk crystals in a plastic bag. When feeding time rolls around, mix 1/3 bottle of crystals with water filled to the 8 oz. line on bottle.

Woops! There goes baby . . . To prevent loss of child from high-chair, simply apply textured appliques (the kind used in bathtubs will do) to the chair back and seat.

How to change the pleat in your slacks: Dip a cloth in solution of 1/4 cup white vinegar and 2 cups water. Wring thoroughly and cover old pleat. Press with low setting on steam iron.

Clogged up sink or tub? To increase the power of your plunger, cover the overflow opening with a cloth. It will provide improved suction.

How to remove wrinkles for velvets and velours: Place in a medium dryer with two or three damp towels and spin away wrinkles. (Never iron — it spoils the pile.)

Plagued by rust in your tool box? Here's a simple way to keep tools rust-free: Just slip a piece of charcoal or chalk (moth balls work too) into the toolbox.

How to remove ceiling stains caused by leaking: Blot the spots with a little chlorine bleach. Repeat more than once for older spots.

Prevent color run-off with new clothing . . . Pre-soak in cool water and vinegar solution.

How to keep rust out of metal lunch boxes:

Line the box with a coating of melted paraffin, careful to cover all the seams.

Be economical: Use only half a dryer sheet for softening fabrics in the dryer. It works just as well.

How can you keep your sectional sofa from sliding apart? Simply insert a small piece of foam or sponge under each leg.

How can you avoid static electricity shocks from your carpet? Simply fill a small vase with water and keep it in the carpeted room.

What to do with left-over carpet scraps? Use them as runners for heavily travelled sections of the room. Or use them as scratching pads for kittens and cats, by tacking a small piece to a wall.

Helpful hints for closets: Always make sure your closets can be opened from the inside as well as the outside, to prevent children from locking themselves in. Always keep closet doors shut. In the winter, open doors mean you are heating an extra space, and in the summer providing air conditioning for your clothes and sweepers.

Cigarette burns in your new carpet? Don't panic. Calmly cut the burned threads with scissors. From the corner of the carpet or in inconspicuous places, cut undamaged threads and glue them into the hole. Cover with paper towels and a book to dry for 24 hours. There . . . good as new.

How to remove indentations from your carpet caused by furniture rearrangement: Apply moisture from a steam iron and brush the nap of the carpet.

How can you clean those tough-to-clean corners of the carpet where your vacuum doesn't seem to pick up? Simply buy an extra toilet bowl brush and use it next to the baseboards and in the corners.

How can you preserve your carpet? The more often you vacuum, the better — and the better you vacuum, the longer the life of the carpet.

How to remove candle wax from the carpet: Scrape off as much wax as you can, using a table knife. Then cover the spot with paper toweling and iron the spot (synthetic setting). The napkin will show through wax. Remove and repeat until all the wax is lifted from the carpet.

Keep candles looking fresh and new. Just rub a soft cloth dampened with rubbing alcohol over the stems.

Never scrape candleholders! To remove untidy wax, simply soak the holders in hot water (provided they are not made of wood).

Woops . . . your candle broke in half! To mend a broken candle, simply hold the two pieces under very hot water (careful not to burn yourself) and melt the wax. Then press the two parts together.

Rearranging your furniture. Be sure to make a scale drawing first, or try making a model of the room and your furniture. Avoid having to move heavy pieces three or four times. And be sure to place old milk cartons or magazine covers under furniture legs, so they slide easily into their new positions.

How to avoid that musty smell in clothing storage bags: Simply keep a fabric softener sheet (the kind you normally use in the dryer) or small bar of fragrant soap in the bag.

Painting tip: When painting window frames or sills, trim the edge of the glass panes with petroleum jelly. Any paint that gets on the jelly will wipe off immediately with a cloth.

How to clean canvas sandals and casual shoes: Spray with carpet cleaner and brush lightly with a toothbrush. Let dry and brush again.

Ironing tip: To prevent creasing the sleeve of your blouse or shirt when you press, simply stuff the sleeve with paper towels before you iron.

Knot in your favorite necklace chain? To untangle, simply place a drop of vegetable oil on the knot and then work out with a straight pin.

How to keep the water level up in your double boiler: Place a few marbles in the bottom of the boiler. They'll let you know when the level is too low, and keep you from ruining the pan.

Soggy tissues? Insert push pins in the four corners of the bottom of the tissue box. Legs keep tissues dry.

New arrivals? If your dog has given birth to a litter, cut strips of cloth for each puppy and place in the bed with the mother. When puppies go to their new homes, send along a strip. It will help comfort the puppy when it misses its mother, and keep it from crying.

How to defrost a refrigerator: As a precaution, your first step should be to unplug the refrigerator. Then cover the floor with towels or rags, or newspapers will do. Remove the contents of the refrigerator and pack in an ice chest — or if you don't have a chest, fill a large garbage bag with ice and put your beverages and food in it. Keep it in the bathtub while you work on the refrigerator.

Next have a garbage can handy for the big chunks of ice that will be breaking away. Do not chip the ice from the walls of the refrig, because you may puncture the freon.

To speed things up, hold a hairdryer in the refrigerator, or fill it with pans of steaming hot water. Then wait.

How can I make my candles last longer? If you store candles in the freezer, they burn longer (and incidently, drip less).

Duplicates in your sewing kit. If you'd like to have a "full service" sewing kit, then try this. Each time you buy thread, rick rack, binding, etc., snip off a little piece and tape it to a card or sheet of paper that you can keep in an envelope in your purse. Then when you go shopping, you'll know exactly what colors of what items you have, and you'll be able to buy according to what you need.

How to light candles on a birthday cake. Using a long fireplace match either start from the inside or the top and work your way through. This way you'll avoid burning the tips of your fingers, scorching your lovely curls and melting your fingernail polish.

How to match wood shades when plastering. Simply mix a little instant coffee with the plaster until you achieve the right shade.

A no tell-tale way to repair knits. If you've ever had a small hole in a knit shirt or skirt, you know that the repairs are almost as fatal as the hole itself. The next time this happens, try repairing the hole with a small patch of lightweight interfacing that's fusible. Just press it onto the wrong side of the shirt or skirt. No more hole.

Let's knot get the thread tangled. Even the most careful seamstress is likely to wind up with tangled thread while sewing. One way to help solve that problem is to work the knotting a little differently. Instead of taking the two strands of thread and knotting them together, knot each strand separately. You'll be surprised at how few tangles you'll have in the future.

Do it yourself dishwasher repair: Before calling a repair service, check to see if

*the dishwasher is plugged in
*a fuse has not blown
*there are no obstructions, such as utensils that have fallen through the racks
*the detergent is flowing freely and not caked to the dispenser

*the hot water heater is working properly
*there are no obstructions to the water filling or draining.

How to get rid of discoloration and stains in the dishwasher: Set a cup of bleach in the bottom of the dishwasher and run it through the entire cycle. Then run a cup of vinegar through an entire cycle. It is very important that you do not mix the vinegar and bleach and cause poisonous gases to invade your dishwasher.

Here's all you do to remove water stains from furniture . . . First, if it is a fresh stain, you can probably remove it by simply blotting and rubbing with a soft cloth. But if not, try a mixture of mayonnaise and cigarette ashes. Rub it in well and let stand a little while before removing.

How to remove scratches from wood top table. There are two methods. First try rubbing the scratch with the meat of a walnut or a pecan. If that doesn't work, take a crayon or eyebrow pencil and fill in the scratched area with a matching color.

How to remove alcohol stains from leather. First, clean the leather with saddle soap. Then apply a scuff-type liquid polish, and try to match the color as much as possible (by testing a small spot first).

Where can I store all my blankets in this small apartment? Lay the blankets out smoothly between the mattress and springs of your bed.

Here's some tips for painters: To prevent

paint from running off your brush down your arm, slit a paper plate and slip the brush through that.

Have to leave in a rush? Put your brush or roller in a well sealed plastic bag. It will stay soft and moist for a while.

Splattered all over? Use baby oil to remove paint from your skin.

When painting the bathroom, remember to cover the tub and sink with wet newspaper, and all the hardware with aluminum foil.

Hints for coping with roach infestation: Roaches love dark and damp places. Be sure to wipe up all spills immediately. Also, thoroughly vacuum behind refrigerators and under the motor, under and behind all furniture, in all crevices (and fill them in with plaster or plastic wood if possible), around all plumbing, under the stove burners, behind all book cases (and it doesn't hurt to occasionally leaf through your books for egg sacs), and across the tops of drapes and blinds. Apply roach spray regularly, or if you prefer mix boric acid and sugar. CAUTION: This mixture is poisonous to kids and pets.

What to do if you are allergic to insect repellants? A number of products will kill itching, stinging insects: Try spray starch, hairspray or deodorant.

Another sleepless night caused by nuisance flies and mosquitoes? Try switching on the night light in the hall or the bathroom light. When the little bugger seeks out the light, close your door.

Yuck! Ants all over my picnic table! Don't panic. Either fill tin cans with water and set the legs of your table in them, or spray insect repellant on old strips of cloth and wrap around the table legs . . . Enjoy.

Should I trade in my dark colored sofa for a more lint-resistant color?

No. just use an old nylon stocking (clean, or course) to remove lint instantly.

Stop that hem from falling. Does it simply drive you crazy to watch your carefully sewed hemline drop because the thread broke? End that problem with this simple technique. About every 4-5 inches, knot the thread in the hemming. That way if a stitch breaks or comes loose it only affects a very small span of the hem.

Soak those sprains away. Sprained ankles and stubbed toes can be soaked in warm water baths for longer periods of time if you use a plastic picnic chest for the bath. The chest will keep the water at the desired temperature, and you'll feel better in no time.

An easy way to work on big bulky items. Making your own curtains or drapes can be a fulfilling project, but working with that much material can be counterproductive to getting the job done. Next time, extend your work surface by setting up your ironing board next to the work table. Set it at the same height and as you need the space, use the board. Big bulky items will sew up faster (or so it seems).

Saving a favorite pattern. It's not much fun to see your favorite pattern wind up in tatters because of overuse. So, if you have a pattern you love, try this. Transfer the pattern, and all its markings, to nonfusible lightweight interfacing. Now you've got a pattern that will work on and on.

An extra organizer in your sewing basket. Tired of binding, rick-rack and elastic getting into a mess in your basket? Straighten up by using leftover spools of thread. Just wind the binding or whatever around the spool and secure it with a pin. You'll have a neat basket and a way to instantly spot what you want. For even more organizing, keep these spools separately in a clear plastic bag.

Basting made even easier. Just when you're getting into the rhythm of those long, easy basting stitches, it always seems that it's time to rethread the needle. End this problem by threading the needle but NOT cutting the thread. Then as you "run out" you just pull more thread through directly from the spool.

Brush those stains out! No, not with a brush, but with toothpaste. That's right, toothpaste! If you have spots or stains on polyester clothing, a little white toothpaste is an excellent way to remove those stains and extend the life of your garment.

Cabbage leaves in your first aid kit. Who would have ever thought that the garden would do so much good for a burn? Believe it or not, cabbage leaves (be sure to wash them thoroughly first) are a soothing agent to minimal skin burns, rashes, etc. Just lay the leaf over the affected area and you'll feel a sense of relief in minutes.

How to keep small utensils from falling to the bottom of the dishwasher: Place a plastic scrubber or sponge in the silverware tray of the dishwasher before filling with the small items.

Homemade scrubbers. Cut old onion or potato nylon net bags into squares and stitch. Fill with a sponge and close the edge. It makes an economical and efficient scrubber.

Ouch! I always burn myself lighting candles. Simply use a piece of spaghetti to light candles.

What can I do with candle nubs? In a coffee can, melt all the scraps together. Insert a wick or just use a string, and you have created your own candle.

What is the best material for potholders and oven mits. The most durable are those crocheted from rug yarn.

How to restore body to limp dacron curtains: Soak them in one gallon of water mixed with one cup epsom salts, and rinse.

Removing adhesives from walls or furniture. Rub some margarine or vegetable cooking oil on the stuck paper or adhesive and carefully remove.

How can I keep aluminum canisters looking clean and new? Silver cleaner will work on aluminum as well as silver.

Homemade furniture polish. Mix equal parts of boiled linseed oil (available in any hardware store), turpentine and vinegar. Voila! What a lustre.

Where to keep messages in an already crowded kitchen: Paint the inside of an cupboard door with chalkboard paint, and you have a perfect message board.

The cellophane caper: If you lose the edge of your plastic wrap, just take a piece of ordinary scotch tape and touch it to the roll until you locate the edge.

Quick Hints:

- In a hurry! An egg poacher is the ideal way to heat up several foods at once.
- Do you love your house plants? Well, bring them into the bathroom the next time you take a shower! They'll thrive in the heat and humidity.
- A stiff wire brush will take the rust off garden wrought iron in a jiffy.
- Need to wash your most delicate lacy items? Just slip them in a small, covered jar with a little cold-water soap and shake them clean.
- Wax your dustpans: dirt will slide right off.
- Cold water and salt are the quickest, surest combination to set color in items you think might fade in the wash.
- Soaked shoes? Save 'em by stuffing them with newspapers to retain their shape as

they dry.

- Your hubbies golf balls can be cleaned easily. Just soak them overnight in a "heavy" solution of ammonia and hot water. No scrubbing, either!
- Always dust oil paintings with a feather duster; never rub a cloth over them.
- Wax your kitchen walls and grease will just wipe off.
- A sponge makes a great soap dish — and its washable!

Do your closets smell? First, never put worn or soiled clothing into the closet. Secondly, keep a small box of opened baking soda in the closet to absorb odors.

Accidents do happen . . . how to remove puppy urine: Quickly sop up as much moisture as possible with paper towels. Time is of the essence. Then blot (don't rub!) the spot with a mixture of 1 tsp. of nonalkaline detergent per half pint of lukewarm water, working from the outside to the inside of the area. Rinse with clear tap water. Lastly, to remove odor, blot the spot with a mixture of 1/3 cup white vinegar in 2/3 cup warm water, and sprinkle with baking soda. Cover with 1/2 inch layer of paper towels weighted down by a heavy book and leave to dry.

How to get rid of fleas from furniture and carpet: Fleas can survive without norishment for several weeks. Therefore, you must first vacuum thoroughly and then apply an insecticide (be sure it doesn't stain). You must repeat this process in a few days to make sure you have destroyed the eggs.

What to do when baby throws up all over parent away from home: Carry a small bottle of baking soda and water in the diaper bag. When baby spits up milk or food, just rub the spot with a cloth dampened in mixture.

How to create more drawer space. Twins instead of one? Try purchasing see-through closet bags with shelves, and use them for things like blankets, sheets, diapers, sweaters, etc.

Fish lovers . . . Don't dispose of aquarium water when you clean your fish tank. Instead, use it to water your plants. It makes an excellent fertilizer.

Can't get that spot out? If it's permanent press we're talking about, simply rub (easy does it!) a little white toothpaste on the stain and rinse. Repeat until the stain is out.

How to get rid of hem lines when lengthening blue jeans: Take a blue crayon and color over the hemline. Cover your ironing board with newspaper or cloth, and iron in the crayon color, by pressing the jeans wrong-side-out.

How to mothproof without a cedar chest. Just wrap your clothing in heavy aluminum foil. Then line a drawer with the same type foil, and fill with moth balls. If the moth balls lose their scent, simply rub gently with a piece of fine sandpaper.

Smelly tennis shoes? Try painting them inside and out with a thick solution of baking soda and water. Repeat as necessary.

Zip-lock bags are your best "friends" when traveling. Use them to keep your shoes from messing up the rest of your luggage.

Or . . . To pick up soiled, delicate underthings, so that they remain separated from your clean clothing.

Or . . . To store souvenirs in (such as shells, postcards, or hotel stationery) when you pack or re-pack during your travels.

Or . . . To pack up sun-tan lotions, medicines, toiletries, or anything liquid and breakable.

Is the pressure getting to you? When traveling by air, it's usually the air pressure that makes you feel weak, dizzy or ill. Because, you see, pressurized cabins cause rapid dehydration. Solution: a couple of glasses of good old H20 down the hatch!

Are your plastic plates and glasses old and scratched looking? Try buffing them up with a little toothpaste! Yes, toothpaste. Use an old toothbrush to apply, and rinse with clear, warm water. It'll remove old scratches and most discoloring, and your plasticware will look new again.

Has your plastic wrap lost its cling? Well, here's a little tip that made our day, and we're sure will make yours, too. Just moisten the rim of your bowl or container, and your plastic wrap will stick just like you always thought it was supposed to!

Chopsticks have many uses. The next time

you get Chinese food, or even order it in, remember to save those chopsticks. They make great plant stakes.

"Eggs-actly" what the cook ordered! Ever been baking away, only to discover you're one egg short for that delicious cake you've already started mixing? Here's a great substitute. Just blend in a couple of tablespoons of real mayonnaise. You'll be the only one who'll know.

Don't burn your fingers with too-short matches when you light candles! Instead, use a piece of un-cooked spaghetti. It makes a great "match", is cheap, and best of all, no burnt fingers.

Do you have an aquarium? The next time you change the water for your fresh-water friends, do your houseplants a favor, too. This fishy water is a real treat for them, and is rich in everything they need. Plus, you'll be "killing" two birds with one stone.

Are your venetian blinds smudged with dirty fingerprints? Here's a great tip: don't wash the entire blind. Instead, use a gum eraser to "erase" those smudged prints, and your blinds will be clean in minutes.

RECYCLING TIPS AND HELPERS

This chapter will provide you with a "second life" for so many of the things that you might have formerly just consigned to the garbage heap! In these days of increasing inflation, everyone is always looking for ways to stretch the dollar as far as it can go. And so, one of the most obvious ways is to take an item that has outlived its purpose in one area, and use it in a totally new way.

We have provided you with creative and different uses for common household substances — such as old stockings, newspapers, tin cans, etc. — and you will be amazed to see what you might have thought of as trash suddenly becoming useful in ways you never imagined. Once you get in the habit of recycling items, you'll wonder how you never thought of these unique ways of transforming "garbage" into productive and useful forms. Not only will it save you money, but it will give you great satisfaction to know that you are not wasting products and in fact, that you are making a great contribution to the ecological health and well-being of the world.

Turn that ordinary box into something special. Have you ever been shopping for children's furniture and been disappointed with the quality? It might be because it was corrugated cardboard. Why pay retail when you can have it for free? The next time you get a box with a top and a bottom, make it into something special. Paint it or glue fabric on it, decorate it with glitter or other notions. You'll be surprised at how you can get an ordinary old box to shine.

Turn caps into cannisters. Plenty of cans come with replaceable plastic tops that turn them into ideal food storage containers. All you've got to do is wash out the can when you've finished with the contents and you've got your container. Or use these same containers to store nails, screws, tacks and other household notions.

Jars on the wall. Now that there are such strong glues available, it opens up a multitude of ways to use them. In the kitchen, you might want to glue several of the same sized jars on the inside of a closet door. Make sure they have air tight caps. Then store whatever you want in them. Because the jars are glass, you can quickly see what's inside. Just unscrew the cap and your goodies are instantly accessible.

Old socks are a great travel companion. Save old socks. The next time you travel, slip one sock over every shoe as a way to protect your shoes and your clothing.

Armwarmers. We all know about those long, wooly tube shaped legwarmers. Do the same thing with old wooly socks. Cut off the foot portion and you've got an armwarmer. Push them up into the sleeve of your jacket for extra insulation from the cold.

Don't waste that last bit of paint. How often have you gone to touch up an area only to discover that the last little bit of paint in the can has thickened — or worse — hardened? Avoid this in the future by taking the last bit of paint and transferring it into a glass jar with a cap. Not only can you see what's there (not to mention how much less space the container takes up), but it's much easier to work with.

Line winter shoes with carpet. It may sound a little weird, but a small carpet scrap makes a great cold weather insulator. Trace your feet on a piece of paper and make a pattern. Then cut out the carpet to fit. Place in rubbers, boots or other winter shoes that could use a little extra help with the cold.

More uses for leftover carpet. Make remnants into small throw rugs which can be used to protect high traffic areas. Or make a matching pet rug for your dog or cat. Carpeting is a favorite device for scratching posts. Staple some scraps to a post for the cat. Use small rug pieces as flooring protection in your auto. Or find a pattern for a carpetbag and make your very own luggage.

Got an old typewriter that needs cleaning? Chew up a few sticks of gum (until the sweetness and flavors disappears). Then use that wad to dab on your typewriter keys. You'll be surprised at how well it picks up lint, eraser dust, even excessive ink on the keys.

Hide it in a book. An easy, and cheap way to hide small items is inside an old book. A hardcover book is best, standard or oversized. Cut out about a 6″ X 4″ hole in the pages (be sure to leave facing pages front and back). Then put in your jewelry, secret papers, or whatever, and place it back on the shelf. No one will ever be the wiser. NOTE: Be sure to remember what book you hid your valuables in!

A bookshelf from old books. Got some old hardcover books that you've finished reading and absolutely no one else wants (that means you couldn't sell them at a flea market, second hand bookstore or anyplace else). Then stack them about 6 high in even heights, put a board across, and you've made yourself a bookshelf from the real McCoy!

A gift that's lucky, too. As the cost of meats keep rising, chicken becomes more popular. And that means more leftover wishbones. Here's another way (besides wishing!) to use them. Dry them. Paint them. Put on a little glitter and tie them to gift packages. The recipients will not only have a nice gift, but have a lucky wish, too.

A throw-away cushion? Absolutely! Ever wish you'd brought a nice insulated cushion along for cold-weather, outdoor spectator sports? Try this trick. Bring along several of your thickest magazines that you've finished reading. Use them as a cushion. You'll find all those pages are a perfect insulator between you and the cold!

When the berries are gone, you can still use the basket. Instead of throwing away a perfectly good plastic mini-basket, try reusing it. It's perfect to catch the scrapings from peeled vegetables (then you can recycle those to the compost heap). Or pack fresh berries in them for the kids' lunch box — these baskets help to keep those juicy little berries from being crushed. Or simply use them for storage.

Keep a windowshade in the trunk. This is a space-saving device that you can be mighty happy to have handy. Use it as a ground throw for an impromptu picnic. Or, if you ever have a flat tire, a window shade can help to protect you and your clothing from the cold, dirty ground.

No more messy paint trays. The next time you've got painting to do that requires a roller and tray, try this. Take a plastic bag and insert the paint tray. Pour the paint into the tray. When you're finished painting, pour the remains back into the bucket (or an old jar if there's just a bit left) and throw out the plastic bag. No muss, no fuss.

Ideas for berry baskets. At holiday time, when you're shipping gifts, help to keep a handsome bow from being crushed by covering it with a berry basket. Or use it as a stabilizer when arranging flowers. Or dry herbs from the garden in them — they have so much ventilation, and they are easy to hang in the sun. If you can't think of another use, refill them with berries the next time you stop at a "pick 'em yourself" roadside stand.

It's more than a security blanket. At today's prices, it's hard to justify ever getting rid of an old blanket, no matter what its condition. If the binding is bad, you can make it look like new again with new edging. If it's more serious than that, cut it down, re-bind it and make yourself a little shawl. If it's really bad, make it into a dog blanket. Rover will love you in the cold winter months.

Try these uses for ties. Make an old tie into a sumptuous belt, or a smashing headband. If the tie is really in poor condition, use pieces of it for an applique patch on other clothes. Or turn a tie into a toy for kids. Stuff it with old stockings and knot or sew shut the ends. You'll have a cuddly snake.

An exercise mat from a scrap. Got a piece of leftover carpet? Cut a segment that's just a little bigger than you are, by about 36″ wide, and you've got an exercise mat that's simple to store and easy to use.

Ironing ease with an old candle. Do you ever wish your iron would slide more easily over the things that need to get the wrinkles out? Try this trick. Lubricate the bottom of your iron by lightly running an old candle stub over its bottom. You'll see that ironing goes faster and easier.

Never throw out an old calendar. The pages of beautifully illustrated calendars make wonderful decorative additions to any gift package. Cut out the picture and paste it down. It's a nice way to give a present that extra touch.

Money from your old cans. Although many people are aware that you can recycle old cans, most don't bother because of the bulk. Why not invest a few dollars in a can crusher? (For those that are more athletic, simply remove both ends of the can, give it a quick rinse, lay it on the floor and stamp it flat. By the way, most kids love to help with this activity.)

Broomstick curtain rods. Lightweight broomsticks are perfect as curtain rods. Save them and cut them down to window size. Then drill holes at either end for mounting (or mount them on pole brackets). Curtains slide easily over these smooth sticks.

Get your money's worth from that old broom. Even if it looks ready for the garbage heap, there's probably a lot of uses for that old broom. Never throw out an old wood handle. It can be used to replace the shafts of broken tools. A broom with its bristles can be placed under a heavy object and used as a dolly to slide the item without scratching the floor. Clean the broom bristles in warm sudsy water. Let them dry in the sun. Then take a handful, twist together at one end with wire, and you've got a handy little crumb broom.

Line your shelves with towels. Somehow for something so obvious, it's too often overlooked. Glue or tack down pieces of old toweling. It's a great way to soundproof your shelving.

Homemade stuffing lends that extra touch. Although everyone saves their bread around holiday time to make turkey stuffing, why not do it all year round? Keep a bag handy and throw in your stale slices. When you've got enough, stuff a roast chicken made from stale bread (it's the best base for stuffing). If you haven't got that much bread around, freeze it once it's stale. Use it for stuffing when you've accumulated enough stale bread.

Make your own drawer organizer. Got a messy drawer that's always out of control? Organize it with leftover boxes. Cut down one to fit the drawer. Then fill it with smaller boxes (the aspirin boxes are perfect) and glue them into the box. Now use it to catch all those pesky items that have a tendency to get lost in any drawer.

A "mattress" for a car mechanic. Did you ever think there must be an easier (and cleaner) way to work under a car. Well, there is. The next time you spot someone throwing out a large appliance carton, save it. The long panels make perfect "mattresses" to slide in and out from underneath your car. That panel will make it easier to slide back and forth, plus it will save on your laundry efforts.

Old sockings have good uses. Fill them with potpourri, tie them and hang them in your closets for an extra sweet smell. Or substitute mothballs and you've winterized your closet. Use old stockings as fillers for pillows and cushions that need a little boost. Try tieing with stockings instead of string. It's just as strong, with a lot more flexibility.

Make it float. If you've ever dropped something overboard, here's a little trick for your next boating excursion. Use the leftover spools from thread as mini-floats for items that could accidentally go astray.

Save that toothpaste tube. When you're finished with a tube of toothpaste, cut off the end, rinse it out carefully and save it, along with the cap. The next time you are using glue, decorating a cake, or need grease for your car repair, pull out your leftover toothpaste tube, fill it, and squeeze.

Tie one on. A stained or worn out tie may look as if it has no more value, but there are still plenty of ways to use it. Cut off the pointed end and make it into a sturdy — but elegant — strap for a bag whose own strap has gone. Turn it into an elegant protective case for a gift picture frame. (Cut off a segment that's longer than the object. Stitch closed the narrow end. Put a snap on the other. Presto.)

Ring around the collar. Instead of pouring spot remover on fabric just before washing clothes (and using more than you need), keep a clean, old vegetable brush with your laundry supplies. Then use the brush to apply the spot remover. You'll see how much further you stretch your liquid cleaner using this technique.

Has this been screened? Old window screens can be used again and again. Save the screening from the worst, and use it for patching on those that need only minimal repair. Or use a piece of screening to prevent debris from clogging an outdoor spout or gutter. If you've got a complete screen use it to dry garden herbs in the sun. Set it on 4 bricks so the air can circulate underneath.

Wallpaper a package. If you've got leftover wallpaper, then you've got the necessary material to wrap up a dramatic gift. Wallpaper makes delightful wrapping paper. And if you've got some old yarn, use that instead of ribbon.

Curlers from your kitchen wraps. Instead of throwing out the cardboard tubes from your kitchen wraps, save them as a beauty aid. Cut them into curler lengths, and use them to make large, soft curls. They are lightweight and will hold easily with a bobby pin.

Sealing mailing tubes. Did you ever wonder how you could recycle those tubes that come inside aluminum foil, wrapping paper, etc. Use them to mail items which are best sent rolled, not flat. Seal them by pinching one side in and pressing the other side firmly down on top. Then seal it permanently with strapping tape.

Try these uses for blankets. If your blanket is in such bad condition that you wouldn't even want Rover to have it, here are some ideas. Use blanket strips as insulation around door jambs and other drafty spots. Wrap furniture in old blankets to protect them when you move. Use them as drop cloths. Or as a dolly to slide furniture across bare floors without scratching. Even your garden plants will love the warmth that comes from insulating with old blanket strips on a frostbitten night.

A decorator's tip that would cost a fortune. It's very chic to accent walls, furniture and other areas with carpet. A decorator would charge a lot of money for that idea. If you've got leftover carpeting, cut it into strips and glue it onto the wall like wallpaper. Or cut out matching seat mats, or face a desk with leftover carpet.

Using everyday household containers. If you've ever watched your garbage fill up with bulky boxes and cartons, you must have wondered about other uses. Here's a few ideas. If you're a camera buff, save the long pasta boxes. They are perfect to store varying size camera lenses. A cut down detergent box is perfect to store back issues of favorite magazines. Lost your dustpan? Cut down almost any lightweight box (a cake-mix box is good) and sweep in the dust. Ask your pizza man for an extra box and use it to store linens to store paper clips, stamps and other little items. Turn your left-over toothpaste box right into a travelling toothbrush holder. Use your tea bag box to get plants started for the garden (just throw in a little wax paper lining). A soup box from dried soups is perfect to store recipe cards.

Candle stubs have plenty of uses. It may look as if there's not another thing to do with those old candle stubs, but they still have plenty of life in them. Melt a few drops of a wax candle and use it to seal an envelope that has lost its stick. Melted wax makes a fine adhesive for any paper surface — use a wax blob to seal gift packages. Throw old stubs into your fire kindling and use them as a firestarter. Rub candle wax on metal runners, inside of drawers — it will help to ease the sticking and make drawers slide better.

Let's get cookin' with grease. Most people throw out leftover fat and grease without ever thinking that it can be reused for many dishes and actually improves the flavor over other available oils. Save bacon grease, chicken fat, etc., but be sure to store each in separate, labelled cans. Cut the beef fat off and give it to the birds. They'll think it's a tasty treat. Use bacon to saute onions, mushrooms and other vegetables. They'll have special flavor.

Make friends with a photography buff. Those 35mm plastic cannisters with tops are ideal for lots and lots of things. Take them on the road and use them for your pills. Keep buttons, clips, screws and other notions in them. In the car you can keep change in them for road and bridge tolls. Use them on your desk to store little items. Or give them to the kids. They'll always find a use for them.

Rags, rags, rags. Even an old rag can be recycled. Take little strips and use them for ties. They are especially good in the garden to stabilize tomato and bean plants. Or use them to tie around the trunks of young trees to protect from the wildlife. You can even use rags to keep a garden warm when an early chill hits. Or use them over bushes for some extra winter protection.

Before you turn a towel into a rag. First you can turn it into a bathmat. Take a couple of old towels, cut out the best parts, and piece them together as a bathmat. Use the leftovers for rags.

Let that take-out burger do double duty. Leftover burger boxes make great aids to keep glasses and cans upright. Just invert the bottom of the box, cut a hole to fit the glass or bottle and insert. The next time the container is accidentally "tapped," it's not likely to fall over. Kids are always impressed with this trick.

From manilla envelope to file folder. The regular 9 X 12 manilla envelope is just a little bit bigger than the standard file folder, but a lot cheaper. Slit down the sides and trim the top and you've got lightweight file folders. Kids especially like these as a way of organizing their drawings, stickers and papers.

A sturdy manilla envelope. If you are sending something that should go flat and you don't want it to bend, put a cardboard shirt stiffener into the envelope. Better yet, tape the envelope to the stiffener and use it as the addressing label. It's a great way to recycle a used manilla envelope.

Don't forget your coupons. Here's a money-saving reason to recycle envelopes. The next time you go shopping, prepare your list on the flap side of an old envelope. Then use the envelope itself to hold all your coupons. With your list and coupons right in hand, you'll find it easier to pick out those bargains.

A hint of a tint and you've got new glasses. Most people don't know that you can take regular clear prescription lenses and have a tint added. So, if you get new pair of glasses, why not have your old, clear pair tinted for the sun? You're likely to find that the dark lens give a fresh look to an old pair of frames.

The cost of tablecloths got you down? Try taking a nice cotton sheet, or one of the decorative, no-iron ones and transform it into a tablecloth. A second sheet can be used to make matching napkins. If you need, cut the sheet down to size with pinking shears. Or if you're really ambitious, sew on a little decorative trim. It's the same thing as a tablecloth, but much cheaper.

Take the juice of one banana skin . . . Would you believe banana skins have juice? Well, to find out for sure, try this bright trick. Cut off the hard ends. Throw the soft pulpy portion of the peel into a processor. Take the banana puree and use it to shine up your silver. You'll be impressed.

When you milk goes bad. There's nothing more disappointing than to get ready for a fresh cup of coffee only to find the milk has gone bad. Don't throw it out in disgust. Save it and use it for milk substitutes in pancakes, waffles and other morning delicacies. Or surprise the family with a homemade sour milk cake. Now that's a treat.

"Leftovers" needn't be a dirty word! If you have a food processor, use it to puree leftover vegetables, meats, and gravies, and then save it to add to the stock the next time you make soup.

Speaking of soup . . . almost any leftover can be added to soup. You'll be surprised just how tasty this "mulligan" stew of leftovers can be!

If your cheese dries out, don't throw it away. Just because it's dry doesn't mean it's spoiled. Simply grate and use as an "au gratin" topping.

Leftover chicken? Of course, you can always make chicken salad. But, have you thought of chicken crepes, pureed chicken spread, or saving the bones, skin and fat for chicken soup?

Here's a great tip for leftover vegetables. Just put the veggies from last night's meal into a frozen pie crust along with any pre-cooked meats, gravies, or left-over potatoes and you'll have a delectable shephard's pie that the kids will always want seconds of.

Leftovers make a great filler. Just use them in an omelette or crepe, and no one will know. This is an especially good idea for leftover cheese, tomatoes, green veggies and any kind of red meat. Seafood makes an especially tempting filler.

The many lives of meat loaf. Try using a variety of left-over meats to make a meat loaf. Your family will love it, and you'll love this money-saving tip.

When "recycling" those leftovers, be clever. Meats can easily dry out. Try making a simple sauce to keep them juicy and able to perk the taste-buds of your finicky family.

Old bananas? Don't pitch them! Why not make banana bread with the over-ripened fruit? And while you're at it, the skin can be used to polish your silver.

Why buy expensive coatings for chicken or fish? Make them yourself. Save an old flour bag, add a little salt, pepper, flour and other spices to taste. Just drop in the fish or poultry and shake.

An old, mis-matched fork can be a help. Keep it close to your favorite houseplants, and use it to "rake" their soil.

Make your own cookie cutters. Simply cut up old frozen food containers, the aluminum ones, into the shapes you want, keeping the sharp edge down.

Here's a great tip for old fruit. Instead of throwing away fruit when it gets a little too ripe, (and your family turns its nose up at it) try this. Cut off all the bad spots and peel the fruit. Use it to top ice-cream, or to bake breads, or best of all, to make an old-fashioned cobbler with.

If none of these ideas thrill you, here's a really inventive one: again, you cut and clean the fruit. Drop the chunks into a large covered jar with a half bottle of brandy in it. Let the mixture set, adding fruit whenever you have it. Soon, in a couple of months, you have a great dessert topping and crowd pleaser for your next party.

Don't toss old ice-cream sticks. They are an invaluable item to recycle for use around the house. They make great coffee stirrers, and you won't have to wash spoons! Use them to "splint" a top-heavy houseplant. Your kids will love them, with a little glue, to build things out of, and you can even use them as markers in your garden. Our favorite, though, is to use them to hold caramel apples in the fall.

Have you saved the lid, but not the jar? Try using them for coasters, as drawer organizers (for thumbtacks, etc.) or to catch the drips off candles.

Old bicycle inner tubes can be used again, too. The "good" portion can be cut and used as rubber bands, and they'll make great slingshots for your kids.

Used, cleaned jars make great organizers. Use them for organizing your sewing basket, work bench or even office drawers. You can even use them to make your own "air-freshener". Just punch holes in the top and fill the jar with potpourri.

Here's another one for an old jar. Let your child cover it in contact paper. Punch a hole in the lid, and "presto"! You've got an "instant" bank.

Large jars have uses, too. Fill them with colored marbles, your cork collections, or even colored water, and they'll make great decorator items to catch light and spruce up your room. "Hide" them among the houseplants, or line your bookshelves with them.

An old knife has value. Especially, the serrated kind. They are great to cut styrofoam or cardboard with, and they make great twig pruners for your small trees.

Aluminum foil goes on forever. It's not exactly cheap, but if you get in the habit of recycling it, you'll find the cost of using aluminum foil is really very inexpensive. Keep a clear plastic bag handy — several are even better — and keep leftover pieces of aluminum foil in them. Sort by size into 3 different bags and it will become even quicker to find the right-sized piece.

A quick greaser. Save your butter and margarine wrappers. (Keep them in a little plastic bag in the refrigerator.) The next time you've got baking to do and the recipe calls for a well-greased pan, just use one of the leftover wrappers to do a quick and easy job.

Dusting by hand. Cut down the time you spend dusting by using an old pair of cotton or wool gloves. Instead of carting around a rag and polish, just run your gloved hands over furniture. The dust collects on the gloves and when they're dirty, just pop them in the wash. Dusting this way also helps you to get into those little dust-collecting crevices!

Recycle that Christmas tree. When you're finished with the tree, cut off all the branches into kindling size pieces. Not only do they make excellent kindling that starts in a flash, but the smell of a pine fire is a delight in the house. WARNING: Use only a few to start a fire since dried pine branches ignite quickly and burn very intensely.

Avoid pine needle droppings from your Xmas tree. Take an old sheet that you might have torn up for rags and use it as a decorative "mat" around the base of the tree. Cut a hole in the center and insert the trunk. When you're ready to remove the tree from the house, wrap it up in the sheet and carry it through. You'll have hardly any pine needles to pick up.

A sponge that does double duty. There's nothing like a sponge, but a sponge inside an old stocking is the best. You get all the benefits of the sponge, plus some extra cleaning power from the texture of the stocking.

Small cans have many uses. Those little cans, the size used for tuna, have many other applications. Once they have been washed, they can be used to reheat small portions in the oven, or used as feeding dishes for your pets, or as organizers for nuts and bolts. With a little imagination, you'll have a big collection of tuna cans.

GARDENING VICTORIES

Growing things is one of the most satisfying experiences that you can have — but if you need help to make sure that your thumb stays "green" — try some of the hints in this chapter. We are sure that you will find that your garden will spruce right up! Whether you have a back yard or just a window box, there are tricks here that will keep your garden growing. From keeping your plants healthy to using used items to enrich your soil — there are a host of tips that will save you money and keep your garden in bloom.

These tips cover the whole cycle of gardening needs — from the initial planting stages through the nursing of plants to make them grow as healthy and strong as possible, to the small tricks that will "make the difference" to your hard toil and effort in the garden.

A reflection of beauty. So many people tend to get their flower arrangements "uneven" when they are finished. The face side looks great, but the back is lacking. If you have that problem, make your next arrangement in front of a mirror. It will give you an ongoing idea of just how well you are doing.

Flowers but no greens. If you have flowers, but no greens, try this. You can break up the flowers into several sparse groupings and place the flowers singly or a few into vases for an oriental effect. Or you can use some fresh parsley or carrot tops for some color. Or if you are lucky enough to have a yard, cut a little greenery from a tree or evergreen.

Long stemmed roses can hurt. Those nasty thorns can be a real blow to the beauty of your hands by the time you've finished an arrangement. If you don't like to wear gloves, use tongs to pick up and place the roses.

Flowers last longer. At the cost of today's flowers, it's nice to be able to extend their decorative lives for as long as possible. Try keeping flower arrangements in the refrigerator at night. Your family will never notice they are gone, and the flowers will live nearly twice as long.

The end of season blues. When the rose season is nearly over, you're likely to wind up with some delectable buds, but not enough to make an arrangement. Pick them as they are ready and keep them in the refrigerator. When you've collected enough for a bouquet, bring them out of the refrigerator. They'll bloom nearly all at the same time.

Half 'n half. Extend your fresh flowers even further by mixing them with some of the beautiful silk ones. (The fresh ones can be kept in flower tubes.) You'll find you can have a dramatic, real-looking arrangement for little money.

A real bonebreaker! Save all those old poultry bones — they make great garden fertilizer. Don't throw away that chicken carcass. Save it.

Let the bones dry and throw into an old burlap bag. When you've got a bunch, crush them with a hammer (or let the kids jump up and down on the bag). Then sprinkle the bones in your garden — or feed them to your houseplants.

Stop those weeds with newspapers. Not only are newspapers a fine mulch for gardens, but they actually stop the weeds from growing, too. Take several sheets, wet them down and lay them on the earth between the rows of vegetables. Weeds won't penetrate. And when the newspaper decomposes, you'll have added a healthy touch to the soil.

Grass seeds and flour. The next time you are sowing seeds, add enough ordinary flour so that the area is "whitened". Then if you have any doubt whether or not you've properly covered the area, you simply look at the flour coverage.

A flower refresher. The next time you buy flowers, put them directly into water (unarranged) and let them stand in the refrigerator for an hour or more. The coolness will put some extra zest back into the flowers.

No more tangled flowers. If you like to arrange flowers, but find they get all tangled up, sometimes even spoiled from being heaped together, this little trick should not only improve the situation but improve the quality of your flower arrangements as well. Place your dish drying rack over a sink filled with water. Let each flower stand in the drainer. There will be no tangling, and you'll easily be able to spot just what you've got and where it should go in the arrangement.

Box those flowers. If you need to take an arrangement on the road, put it in a grocer's box. Put newspaper around the sides to hold it firmly in place. Water it as soon as you reach your destination.

Skate through the job. Have you ever envied kids flying down the street on a skateboard? Well, here's an opportunity to put one (safely) to good use. If you're trimming a sidewalk, driveway or other hard surface, sit on a skateboard as you trim. Instead of crawling along, you can glide along on that board.

A flowering vegetable garden keeps out the wildlife. If you're plagued by deer, rabbits and other wildlife and it's ruining your vegetable garden, try a few of these tricks. Plant a solid border of marigolds (they don't like the smell). Or plant garlic as a deterrent.

Prune and tote. If you've got a lot of pruning to do, put plastic sheets (or old sheets) down around the bushes. When the pruning is through, "bag" the clippings inside the sheets and toss away. It's a lot faster (and less painful) than that constant bending over to pick up the clippings.

Shine up your plant leaves. Most people know it's good to dust off the plant leaves. But it's generally such a chore that the job is overlooked. Here's a way to make the job extra quick. Moisten a paint brush. Gently brush the leaves. It's surprising just how fast you can shine up your leaves with this technique.

Stop knee pain when gardening. Cut out a piece of soft foam and use it as a knee mat. Or wear knee pads. Or wear old stockings with a little foam insert at the knee.

Ashes to ashes . . . Cleaning out the fireplace may seem like a pesky, dirty thing to do, but when you consider the value of the ash, the task may seem a bit more appealing. Next time, save the ash (a metal container is best — in case of live embers) and use it as a way to control the pH level in your garden. Ash is rich with phosphorous, potash and other elements. Sprinkle it liberally over your garden in the late Fall. You'll have a healthy garden in the Spring.

Garden and have clean nails. If you don't wear gloves, but hate the look of your nails after the job is finished, give them some extra protection with ordinary soap. Dampen the bar and then dig in. The caked soap under your nails will keep out the dirt.

Spray your plants and protect the furniture. Every gardening tip book tells you to spray your plants — they love the moisture. But what about the furniture. Spray is not so good for wood. So try this. Hold several sheets of newspaper behind the plant (but close to it) and the spray will stop at the leaves. No more wiping furniture dry.

Removable ivy! There's nothing more beautiful than an ivy covered house, but we all know it can play havoc with the exterior walls. That's why smart homeowners use a climbing trellis beside the house so you can get the same effect, without the problems. But what happens when you go to paint? That darn trellis is in the way. If you hinge it at the bottom, you can simply pull it away the needed inches to get at the house.

A "holey" hose can be put to good use. To buy a good soaking hose (with the little holes) can be quite expensive. If you've got a hose that's no good because of leaks, turn it into a soaking hose. Just punch some more holes along the length and you're ready to put it to good use.

Free chives. If you're like most people, green onions are used for the upper green portions in your cooking. But if you save the bottom part (the bulb, plus 3/4 inches) you've got a little plant in the making. Just pop it into a pot, water it and let it grow. Snip off the green parts as you need them.

"Bottle Sitters" for your plants while you're away. If you'll be vacationing for a while and are worried your plants will run out of water, try this. First water them thoroughly. Then, for every plant fill a plastic bottle with water (use leftover 2-liter soda bottles for big plants and the 1-liter bottles for smaller ones). Punch two holes in the lower sides. Then place one bottle per plant into the soil. Let the water drip in while you are away.

If you must smoke, then here's a healthy tip. It's hard to imagine that there is a genuine use for a cigarette butt, however, it makes a wonderful pesticide for mealbugs (a favored pest of the house plant). Here's all you do. Empty the tobacco from an ashtrayful of butts. Soak the tobacco for 24 hours. Strain out the water and save it — discard the tobacco. Put the tobacco water in a container and spray it on the affected plants. It's a real killer.

Water water everywhere. One of the biggest mistakes that amateur gardeners make is to water regularly — but not enough. Unless you have the time to water thoroughly (that means soaking the ground to at least 1 inch in depth) wait until you can do it. Continuous, light waterings will force the roots upward and weakens them to the point of dying. (This same thing holds true with houseplants.) Water once a week or 10 days if you must, but make sure you've soaked the ground.

More plant fertilizer. We all know that crushed eggshells are a favorite fertilizer. But here's a shortcut. Soak your leftover eggshells in a covered container for 24 to 36 hours. Feed the plants the water and throw out the eggshells.

Keeping flowers fresh. Another way to get extra life from your fresh cut flowers is to remove the leaves that will be submerged in water and cut the flower on an angle. Then scrape the stem a little.

Clean up outside. Keep a bar of soap tied into an old stocking which is hung beside the hose. When clean up time comes, family can wash their hands without ever removing the bar of soap from the stocking. Rinse and they're ready to come indoors.

There's always something to do with an eggshell. Almost everyone knows that eggshells are a perfect addition to a garden "feed" or a compost heap. But here are some other great uses. Dried and crushed fine, they are a perfect mineral supplement to cat or dog food. Or use half the shell as a mini-pot to start seedlings. It's a healthy place for them to live — not to mention that you can plant the "pot." You can even make a simple glue from eggshells. Beat them in a blender with one egg white until they form a gritty paste. Not the word's greatest glue, but fine for paper and the kids will love it.

End crooked hedges. If you've ever spent a lot of time pruning, only to discover that you did it crooked and have too much "touching up", then string a straight line from end to end (use a leveler if you need to) at the proper height. Then prune down to the level of the string.

Tired of scratched up hands from heavy garden work? There's nothing more unattractive than hands that look as if you've been training lions because of the scratches. If you don't like protective garden gloves, then try using over-sized tongs to hold the branches. Then cut with the other hand.

Salvage that bouquet. If you have an arrangement that's basically finished, examine it before you throw it out. You're likely to find at least a handful of flowers that still have life. Save those and add a little greenery. You'll have a new arrangement.

My flowers are too short for the vase. If you've got a favorite tall vase and somehow the flower stems are always too short, try this. Buy several dozen green marbles (like kids use). They are best if they are plain. Put them into the base of the vase until the flower stems reach the marble "bottom". Because they are green, you'll hardly notice they are there.

A healthy meal for houseplants and favorite shrubs. From now on, whenever you cook or steam vegetables, save the leftover water. When it cools, feed it to a houseplant, or give it to a favorite shrub or tree outdoors. They'll love the vitamins. You can also save coffee grounds, or leftover black coffee or plain tea and give them that.

Unruly houseplants. If you have ivy and other hanging plants and they tend to get too long but you hate to cut them, try this. Pin them back into the soil with a hair pin (U-shaped). Eventually they will root, giving you a much more lush plant.

Weak stems. If you're ever faced with a flower arrangement that droops, try boosting the stems up with green straw inserts. A half-dead arrangement will suddenly come to life.

Find a permanent home for your fern. Although ferns are easy to care for, most people don't realize that they like to have one spot in which to live. So don't move them around in your home. Find one place and keep them there.

Leftover hair? What next? If you regularly clean out your brushes and throw out accumulated hair, try this. Save the hair and stuff it into old stockings and panty hose. Knot each end so that the hair is secured in a wad. Tie these "hairballs" to young trees or bushes that deer and rabbits favor. The scent of humans from the hair scares away wildlife. P.S. If you live in the country where deer are a real problem, get leftover hair from your barber shop.

Your very own compost heap . . . Everybody talks about compost heaps, but did you ever wonder what should really go into one? Here are some suggestions: coffee grounds . . . all leftover fruits and vegetables . . . plant cuttings and stalks . . . mulched up leaves . . . cut grass . . . any spoiled fruits and vegetables . . . all peelings . . . eggshells . . . rinds . . . wood chips, etc. Leave out animal fats and anything that isn't biodegradable.

Planting with styrofoam. What do you do with all those wonderful little styrofoam "peanuts" that come packed into cartons so often nowadays? Besides their obvious shipping re-use, why not use them as drainage the next time you're replanting house greenery. These "peanuts" are extremely lightweight, yet tough, so they'll hold up under that earth and provide great drainage.

Flowers got a headache? Cut flowers will remain fresher longer if you do any of the following: Put an aspirin in the water each day. Put a tiny bit of bleach (1/4 teaspoon) into the water. Change the water each day.

Plants in the bathroom. Most people don't think of the bathroom as a place for plants — especially if it's an interior room. However, plants love the humidity and a plant light can provide the "sunlight." Or, treat a plant to the humidity and keep it in the bathroom for a week. It will love all that moisture.

An easy way to babysit your plants. If you're going away for 14 days or less, try this. Put your plants in the tub with just enough water so that the pot does NOT get soaked in water. Cover the tub with a plastic sheet or dry cleaning bags. (Be sure to water the plants just before you leave.)

Old seeds with new life. Last year's seeds (or the year before) got you wondering whether or not they are still any good? Test them with this trick. Count out 60 seeds. Lay them out flat on a sheet of wet newspaper. Cover with another sheet of wet newspaper and cover with a plate or lightweight pan. Wait 4-5 days. Then count the number of seeds that have sprouted. If most did not germinate, throw away. If 50% or more germinated, adjust your coverage to compensate. (Half germinated, use twice as many seeds, etc.)

Water change for big arrangements. It's hard to change water in a large arrangement without disturbing the entire thing. So here's one way to do it. If you can, tilt the vase and pour off as much water as possible into the sink. Then drain off more with a turkey baster and add fresh water. If the vase is too big to tilt, drain as much as you can with a baster and add fresh water.

Flower power. If you are conscientious enough to change the flower water every day (or nearly so), try using warm water instead of cold. The flowers drink it up faster and it will freshen up that bouquet.

Cloudy water is a thing of the past. If you love to show off your crystal and clear glass vases, but don't like the cloudy water, here are a few things you can do about it. Strip the leaves that will be submerged. This will cut down on plant rot. Change the water every day. Or, try 1 tablespoon of household bleach to each quart of water.

The low cost of potting plants. If you are ever dismayed about how much flower pots cost, then here's how you can pot for free. Save your old 2-liter plastic soda bottles. Cut them down to size. The ones with the black plastic support at the bottom are especially good. Before planting, punch a few holes in the bottom for drainage (a heated pick will do this the quickest). These pots are great for children to work with.

Are you an avocado lover? Save the pits and start a plant. If you don't like to go to the trouble of "water starting" them, just pop the pit into the earth of an existing houseplant. Once it has a root system, transplant it to its own pot.

CLOTHING CARE TIPS

Everyone loves their clothing, and all of us know that the image we present to the world is an important one. Because of these facts, we've compiled another chapter on the "care and feeding" of your wardrobe. Unlike its predecessor in volume I, this incisive chapter deals with specialized items and problems, such as how to care for your designer jeans and keept them new looking longer, or the best way to hand wash your daintiest, frilliest "personals". We'll show you how to extend the life of your clothes, and keep them lovely, too.

Automatic hand washables. Unless they are extremely delicate, you might try washing your hand laundry on the delicate cycle of your machine, using very mild detergent. Then hand dry, or put in the dryer for just a few minutes. Remove while the articles are damp. (Don't wash stockings and pantyhose this way unless you have them in a protective bag.)

Washing hand laundry. If your family gets annoyed to find the sinks filled with soaking hand laundry on wash day, here's a way to get the job done and keep the sinks free. Get a small plastic bucket or basket and use that to soak the wash. Leave it in the tub. But if someone wants to take a bath, just set it on the floor. Use the bucket between washdays to store your hand washables like a hamper.

Hasty hemline repairs. If you've ever been in a situation where you discover your hem is sagging, or the lining hangs below the skirt, try some double-sided tape to hold it right back up. If no double-sided tape is available, make a strip of tape into a circle and use it double-sided that way. No tape available and it's an emergency. If it's a lining, or jeans, staple them back as a temporary measure.

When Fido's been bad on the rug. Make sure you get all that odor out so he doesn't repeat the accident. While the stain is still wet, sprinkle on plenty of baking soda. Leave it for several hours, or until dry. Then vacuum up the soda and all the odor will be gone.

A kick in the old down. The next time you wash your down jacket or vest, try this snappy way to get some real fluff into that jacket. When you throw it into the dryer, put in an old sneaker. The sneaker will beat the jacket fluffy.

Make your own fabric softener. The little fabric softener sheets that we throw in the dryer are just great, but they are also expensive. Here's a money-saving way to accomplish the same thing. Take just a little of the liquid fabric softener you would use in your wash and dab it onto a washcloth. Then throw it in the dryer. You've got your own fabric softener sheet.

For heavy clothes, use heavy hangers. Bulky winter clothes often need good sturdy hangers. Wooden ones are expensive. Instead, take two or three hangers and tape them across the bottom and at the neck. You'll have a nice bulky hanger for your clothes.

Fabric softener sheets have another use. If you are like so many people who don't like to clean lint traps with your hands, try this. When you're finished drying clothes, take the fabric softener sheet and use it to pull off the lint from the trap. Then throw them away together.

Cut some of those clothing wrinkles. Many people question why their clothes come out of the dryer so wrinkled—even when the clothes are immediately removed. Often it's because the dryer is overpacked and the clothes don't have room to "fluff." If you're faced with this problem, try putting less clothes in the dryer.

Cold hands, cold wash. If you're an outdoor enthusiast and hang your clothes to dry outside in the winter, here's a way to keep your hands a bit warmer doing the chore. Fill a hot water bottle with hot water and throw it into the basket. Each time you grab for another item, just give that bottle a warming squeeze.

A quick pick-up for your shoes. Most business people will tell you that it's very important that your overall appearance be good—including your shoes. So next time you're at the office and you notice your shoes could use a little shine, rub in a dash of handcream and buff (keep an old powder puff handy—it makes a great buffer).

White shoes look whiter. Have you ever hesitated to buy white shoes because you're afraid of what the scuff marks will do. This summer season, get a bottle of white typewriter correcting fluid. (If you don't work, it's available at almost any stationery store.) The correcting fluid comes with its own little brush. Just white-out the scuff marks and then polish.

For those gold and silver shoes. We all know how popular gold and silver shoes have been, so I'm sure you've experienced your share of disappointment over the scuff marks. Get rid of them as quick as 1-2-3 with a touch-up like you were brushing your teeth. Use an old toothbrush and some white tooth polish. No more nasty scuff marks.

Tar on your car? If you've ever driven by a road crew only to discover that you've got tar on your car as a result, here is an easy way to remove it. Make a paste of baking soda. Take a sponge and apply gently. That hard-to-remove tar will come right off.

A remedy for that hole in the pocket. Somehow that last stitch breaks just at the most inopportune time. If you're faced with a hole in the pocket and you're away from home, try this remedy. Empty out the pocket and turn it out (or take off the item and work from the inside). Twist a rubber band tightly around the hole and you've got a perfect pocket again.

Get rid of that crease mark. If you are faced with lengthening clothes, but can never quite get rid of the original crease mark, then try a little white vinegar as an aid. Dampen the crease mark liberally with the vinegar. Then place a damp cloth over the crease mark and press with a hot iron. No more crease.

Clean up a messy button box. No house is complete without a button box (especially one that gets passed on to the next generation). But have you ever noticed how unorganized they tend to be? Here's a few ways to clean up a messy button box. If you've got lots of identical buttons (like those from shirts), thread them onto the wire twist ties and twist the wire closed. Or use two strips of scotch tape and lay them down in a layer and cover over with the transparent tape. Or put matching buttons in little baggies. Oversized buttons in another baggie. Strange buttons in still another.

An easy way to hem jeans. Although there is nothing hard about hemming jeans, there is something that is very hard about getting that needle in and out of that heavy material. Here's the "loafers" way to do it. Turn them up and tape them with the silver duct tape that you can get in any hardware store. It lasts washing after washing. And if the jeans shrink a little, it's easy to readjust the hemline.

Update a jacket or blouse. A favorite blouse or jacket can have a whole new look just by changing the buttons. Go through your button box and see if you've got anything smashing left over from years ago. If not, invest a few dollars in "knock-out" buttons and you'll have a different jacket or blouse.

Sew a button so it stays on. There is nothing more annoying than sewing a button only to have the thread wear out so the button needs care again. End this problem by sewing with dental floss (nylon fishing line will do the same thing). If you need a different color, use the floss, then finish the job by using a little matching thread to cover over the white. You won't have to re-sew that button.

Organize your clothes sorting. One way to cut down time spent with your laundry is to sort by family member. If family members are old enough, have a pre-designated "pick up" spot where they can get their clean laundry. Let them put it away. If too young to help out, sort it and then bring it to the room.

End messy threads when you sew. For many people, cleaning up after there's been any amount of sewing going on is always a chore. It will go much faster if you keep a little plastic bag or baggie by your side. Just pop in threads, old spools in the garbage before it has a chance to go astray.

Save those dungaree knees. If you're a mother with young, active kids, you probably feel as if they are making holes in the knees before the jeans even get out of the store. To give those jeans a better chance, iron in patches in the knee on the INSIDE of the jeans. No one will see them and they'll increase the life of the knee of that jean. When they wear through, double patch them.

Sharpen those scissors. There's nothing

worse than a dull pair of scissors, but unless you've paid a lot of money for them, it's hardly worth taking them to be professionally sharpened. Next time they get a little dull, take a steel wool pad and buff the edge. Be careful, though.

A trick for designer jeans. It used to be that jeans were the cheapest thing you could buy. Now that designers have broken into the field, jeans often require elaborate care. The next new pair of expensive jeans should be washed in the following manner. The first time, soak them for 2 hours in cold, heavily salted (3 tablespoons per gallon) water. This will set the dye. Then wash, using the cold-water setting.

Sweater touch up. The next time your sweater looks a little shabby around the cuffs and waist, dip them into hot water, blot excess water with a towel and dry with the hot air from a blow dryer. They'll shrink back to size and make the sweater look fresh again.

An easy way to block sweaters. When it's new (or fitting perfectly) outline the sweater on an old framed screen. Make the outline in white chalk. Once you've washed your sweater, "block it" to fit the outline. Put the screen up on bricks so that the air circulates, and you've got the perfect way to dry that sweater. (Or rest the screen over the tub to catch drippings.)

Scuff marks? Erase 'em. When it's spring, a young girl's fancy is likely to turn to light colored shoes. They're beautiful when they are brand new, but oh, so shabby with scuff marks. Next time you're faced with this problem, get an art-gum eraser (available at stationery stores) and erase the marks. You'll be pleased with the results.

Stocking bags. If you wear colored stockings, here's a trick to help you organize. Sort your stockings into clear plastic bags. Keep knee-hi's in one bag, colored stockings in another, opaque in another, beige in another. Not only does this help to access stockings and panty hose more quickly, but the bags protect them for snagging in the drawer.

Tired of grey looking lingerie? Next time this happens, give them a little color lift. Don't worry about the dye, it's easy. Make up some hot, strong, strong tea and soak them until your lingerie is just a little darker than desired. Give one quick rinse in cold clear water and the dye is set—and so are you—with fresh, new looking lingerie.

Do your bra and slip straps slip? Here's two ways to stop that slipping. First, you can sew little snap loops into your dresses. Slip the loop under bra and slip and snap on the other side. An even faster way is to sew a lightweight elastic strip from one strap to the other. You'll never know it's there except that your straps stop slipping.

A new way to dye faded old jeans. If you'd like to give those old jeans a fresh, new look, but don't want to go to all the trouble of dying, try this. The next time you buy new jeans, wash them several times with your old faded ones. The dye from the new jeans will give those old ones a big pick up.

Better steaming power with vinegar. If your steam iron goes into a slump every once in a while, try running white vinegar through it. Let it steam until the big bursts are over. After the iron has cooled, pour out the vinegar. Then rinse the iron throughly with water. You'll find your iron has new life and generates lots more steam.

Make your ironing even faster. If you immediately hang things up when you take them out of the dryer, they won't have the opportunity to get extra wrinkles from being piled in a basket. Ironing will go a lot faster because you'll have less to do.

Run out of fabric softener? The next time that happens, don't despair. Just take a little of your own cream rinse and add it to the wash. Your clothes will come out soft and fluffy.

Air your clothes. If you wear an item of clothing which you plan to wear again, hang it up immediately, then "air" for several hours or overnight. Most of the wrinkles will have hung out and it will be aired and ready for a second wearing.

Clean blankets with a professional look. If your blankets can be machine washed, here's a way to have them looking at their best. Before washing the blanket, set the cycle, add the detergent and let the machine fill. When all the soap is dissolved, add the blanket. Let it soak, and then wash on gentle. In the final rinse, add 1½ cups of white vinegar. It will give your blanket a clean smell, and give it a little fluff.

Softening up those new jeans. One way to do it is to wash them a few times before wearing. But try this energy-saving trick. Take a big bucket or garbage can (make sure it's a clean one) and soak them overnight (or for 12 hours) in cold water with plenty of fabric softener. Then wash as usual.

New life for an old straw hat. Soak it in cold, salt water until it's nice and soft and moldable. Then shape it back to its original condition and let it dry.

What happens when clothes aren't colorfast? Always check the label. If it doesn't say colorfast, be prepared that the color will run. That means taking some action steps. The first few times, wash these clothes separately from your other wash. And try this tip for "setting" the color: Soak non-colorfast clothes in cold water for two hours with ¼ cup white vinegar per gallon of water. It'll help to set the color.

Taking the colorfast test. If you have new garments that you're not sure are colorfast, try this simple test. Wet a clean, white rag or lightcolored cloth. Wring it out and rub over an inside seam of the garment. If the color stays set, it's colorfast.

A money-saving tip for concentrated liquid detergents. Keep a plastic cup handy by the machine. Use it for measuring. When you've poured in the liquid, throw in the cup, too. The wash will pick up all the excess that was left in the cup—and you'll always have a clean cup with which to measure.

Out of detergent, but overwhelmed with dirty clothes? One of the great all time cleaners is powdered dish-washer detergent. It will get your clothes clean, sparkling and bright (just like your dishes). Use 1/4 cup per load. However, don't use this detergent unless your washables can stand a little bleaching, too.

TRAVELING AND VACATION HINTS

Everyone knows that you can have a wonderful time with your family when you go camping, go on vacation, or travel to a new and distant spot. However, sometimes disaster can set in—when you suddenly find that you have forgotten to bring along an important item, or you encounter bad weather and the children are fussing and difficult to amuse, or things don't go quite as you had planned. We have collected a whole range of hints in this chapter designed to see you through the problems that might arise. Everything from tips on substitute products when you camp, to precautions to make sure your take, to special ways to pack when you travel that will enable you to make sure that you don't arrive in your new vacation spot with clothes that are crushed beyond wearing, and have to spend half of your vacation washing and ironing your wardrobe! These tips should go a long way towards making sure that your leisure time is spent trouble-free, and that you and your family can have a truly enjoyable camping or travel experience.

Try this easy way to keep your car free from clutter when you travel with your child. Take a shoe bag and hang it over the back seat of the car. This will serve to hold small toys, bottles, crayons, and other favorite items in the pockets. You'll have a neater and more pleasurable trip.

Does your child clamor to jump into the

pool as soon as you arrive at your motel? Try this easy trick. Tuck your child's swimsuit in a separate plastic bag and keep it handy. That way, you won't have to unpack all your luggage in order to find it. Your child will be able to have instant fun in the water!

Try this new way to provide a sleeping area for your child when you travel. Store your suitcases on the floor of the car of the back seat. Then take a baby mattress and spread it across them to make a level "floor" with the car seat. Then add a quilt across and you'll have a great area for your baby to sleep or play in during your stops. One warning: be sure your baby has a protective restraining device, such as a halter or seat belt when you travel.

Do your older children get bored easily when you take a trip? Try this game to keep their attention. Give each child a map of the United Stated and a colored pencil. Then, as you drive, they can keep a lookout for cars with license plates from the different states. When they see one, they mark that state in pencil on the map. They'll have fun keeping an eye peeled for new states, and this will also reinforce the location of the states.

Try this way to have a picnic whenever you're ready, even if there's no picnic table available. Pack a folding TV tray in your car trunk. Then, when you stop for your picnic, just set it up and you'll have a portable picnic table no matter where you are!

Are your children constantly thirsty when you travel, no matter how many times you give them a drink? Try this easy tip. Instead of giving them water, give them a cup of crushed ice. This will keep them busy longer, too. All you have to do is keep a cooler chest full of crushed ice and some disposable cups inside the car.

Try this trick to keep your children from getting restless while you wait for a restaurant order of food to arrive. One parent should go inside and place the order for everyone in the family. The children can then play outside with the other parent, and when the order comes, all go inside.

When you're camping, does your toddler stray easily? Try this way to provide ID just in case. Take some twill tape and make a wrist band for your child. In indelible ink, write out the full name of the child, plus the number of your lot and campsite. If you can let your child know that it is really important for her to keep this band on, you'll certainly lessen the chance of her getting lost.

When you're driving, do your children fuss around so that you find yourself turning around to intervene? Here's a way to lessen this potentially dangerous situation. Clip an extra mirror on your dashboard or on the sun visor of the car. That way, you'll be able to easily see the action in the back seat, and you can give your instructions without having to keep turning around.

When you travel, do you find that your chil-

dren always arrive dirty? Try this to have them spic and span when you arrive at your destination. Take along a bottle filled with a little soap and water, plus a washcloth and towel. Then, just before you arrive, stop to wash their faces and hands. This will ensure that your children will arrive clean and ready for a visit.

Does your child keep spilling his drink when you ride in the car? This simple trick will help. Instead of using a regular cup, try a training cup that has a lid and spout on it. This will prove fun even for an older child, and it does a fine job of preventing spills.

If you're bothered by the sand that your family tracks in after being at the beach, try this way to solve the problem. Take some damp washcloths along and put them in a plastic bag fastened by a twist tie. As you approach the house, have the kids wipe their feet off with the washcloth and then just put it back in the bag. You'll eliminate most of the sandy mess this way.

Are you tired of having to wait for room service when travelling, because you just can't wait for your morning coffee? This will help. Take along an electric coffee pot or a hot pot to heat water in. That plus some instant coffee will give you coffee just as soon as you want in the morning—and you'll save some money, too!

Try this trick to protect your suits when travelling if you don't have a garment bag. Just button up the clothing inside an old raincoat or layer up several plastic bags from the dry cleaner.

When you place dresses in the back seat of your car, do they hang down and drag? Try this easy way to prevent the problem. Put cardboard tubes on the hangers and then place your dresses across the hangers just as if they were pants. They will hang just right, and won't drag on the car floor or wrinkle.

Here's a tip to make driving easier when you are alone and trying to follow a map. Write out your travel route before you start your trip. Then pin the route to the seat of your car or place it on the dashboard with tape. This will not only make your job easier, but much safer, since it is really dangerous to try to drive and read a map at the same time.

Do you take a lot of vitamins? How can you get your supply, yet avoid taking along all of the large bottles when you travel? Count out the number of pills for the days you will be away, and then take only those you will need in a small bottle or plastic bags. That way, you'll avoid having to carry bulky bottles.

Here's a way to prevent your clothes from arriving wrinkled when you take a trip. Just roll your clothes instead of packing them straight across. Another way is to pack with lots of plastic bags—to provide air—and place the heavier items in the bottom of the suitcase. This should avoid the wrinkles every time.

Are you always running out of room when you pack? This will help. Roll your belts, ties, and small items and instead of packing them in the suitcase regularly, just slip them inside your shoes. This will use the space wisely, and you'll be able to take along more.

If your suitcase is lost, how can you remember what you've lost? Whenever you go on a trip, it's a good idea to prepare a list of all of the articles in your suitcase. That way, in case the suitcase is lost, you'll be able to give a complete list. Since you must provide this to the carrier, you'll be able to do this easily and it will save lots of time and trouble. Just carry the list in your purse or pocket.

When you look for one small item in your suitcase, do you disarrange everything else? Try this trick. When you pack, place everything in large plastic bags. Put shirts in one, shoes in another, and toilet articles in yet another. Then, in order to get at what you need, you just have to slip out one bag, and everything else will remain neat and in order.

When you travel, do you end up with not enough to wear? Or with clothes that you never wear? Try this plan to eliminate this problem. Before you go, make out a "clothes menu". Figure out what you are going to wear for each day that you will be away. Then—mix and match all the clothes so that you work within the same color scheme—and your accessories will work even harder for you.

Do you always forget one item when you go away—like your navy belt or your white bag?

Here's a way to beat the problem. Before you go, write out a master list. Start from the bottom up—with shoes, stockings, etc. and work your way up. Then, when the list is finished, use it to pack from. You'll find that you always have just what you need.

Do you have to dump out everything in your bag when you go through security? Try this plan for making life simpler. When you pack your purse, put everything into several small plastic bags. Then, when you go through Security, just pull out the bags, instead of having to dig around through everything. It will save lots of time, trouble, and embarrassment!

When you travel, are you caught short when you need an emergency clothing repair? Try this. Put some safety pins and a few needles that are pre-threaded inside your suitcase—that way, in case your hem comes undone or you lose a button, you'll be ready to do a quick and instant repair.

Are you tired of having to pack all those big bottles of toiletries every time you travel? Here's a way to make life easier. Buy sample-sized toiletries and leave them already packed in your suitcase. That way, when you have to travel, you'll be all set.

Just before you pack to leave, are you faced with a wet toothbrush? Here's a way to travel nice and dry. Just take your hair dryer and use it to blow the toothbrush dry. That way, you'll always be packing a dry brush.

Try this easy way to avoid exposing your vacation film. When you travel, be sure to pack your film in the suitcase which you are shipping. That way, the film will not have to be put under the X-ray machine, avoiding possible exposure and ruin of the film.

Does your clothing slip around when you travel with a garment bag? Try packing this way. First place your hanging garments in the garment bag, then fill the bottom with sweaters and heavier items. These will serve to hold everything in place, and you'll travel without slipping.

This easy secret will keep your garments in good shape when you travel. Use some tissue or some old dry cleaning bags and as you pack, insert it between each garment. You will supply air pockets, which will keep your clothes fresher and crease-free during your travels.

Does your soft luggage need a little extra form? Sometimes it's nice to reinforce the bottom of soft luggage. So on your next trip, you might want to cut out an insert from cardboard and lay it into the bottom of your luggage. Not only will it give it a little extra form and strength, but it will act as a protector to the bottom layer of clothes in case your luggage is placed in a wet area or on damp ground.

Belt up your suitcase. Have you ever picked up your luggage from the conveyor belt at an airline only to discover that the locks burst in transit and many of your personal items have been lost or damaged? Here's a simple trick. Take an old leather belt and wrap it around your suitcase as an extra safety device. A strong leather belt is a great way to keep a suitcase together, even if there has been a problem while travelling.

Keep toiletries together. Once the toothpaste gets lost on a camping trip, it becomes a problem that affects the whole family. Keep all your toiletries together in a see-thru baggie or in a zippered overnight kit. That way there's one bag to carry and keep organized.

Home Sweet Home. Most tents tend to look alike (and cabins, too), so try this. Identify your place with a flag or other item that is outstanding in color or appearance. Then when the kids are hunting for your place, they'll know just where to look for you.

Those camping showers. A sodden camping trip can be a real downer. Even if it rains for just a brief time, it can really dampen the trip. So buy a plastic garbage can with a tight-fitting lid. Keep all the paper supplies and other things in it that could be ruined if the rains and wind suddenly came along. It's also a great way to get and stay organized.

A plastic pillowcase. Much as you wouldn't think it, this is also a camping essential. Keep your clean clothes zippered inside the case and you'll never have to worry about moist, soggy things, (or any little critters for that matter).

Plastic shopping bags are an essential. If you've ever been disappointed with the space allotted for your towels and clean clothes at the camp shower, tote them along in a plastic shopping bag. Just hang up the bag and you'll have everything you need at your fingertips. Plus the bag will keep things dry.

The camping satchel. Because it's so easy to forget an essential (and usually very inconvenient to buy it any place) try making up a special satchel that carries all the essentials. Everything that is non-perishable remains in the satchel. For those things that must be added, keep a checklist in the satchel. Then you'll know exactly what to go for.

Save that last inch of liquid detergent. Bring a nearly finished bottle of liquid detergent with you on your next trip. At the camp site, fill it with water. This trick gives you a soapy water dispenser for quick clean-ups. And you can dispose of it before you go.

Campware. Most people can't justify buying a complete set of plastic, portable dishes for camping. On the other hand, paper plates and cups get pretty expensive. Start a box that's filled with dishes you get from tag sales, or one-of-a-kind dishes from store sales, etc. Pretty soon you'll have a complete collection that will have cost you only pennies.

Travel size toiletries. Save the travel size shampoo and lotion containers and simply refill. But for things like toothpaste, soap and deodorant, save the "last bit" of each and keep for your next trip. You'll have just enough for the vacation without having spent good money to buy small sizes.

Eat first, camp later. By the time you've packed, travelled, and settled in, it's often too late, or you're just too tired, to begin cooking a meal by the campfire. Next time you go camping, prepare the first meal before you ever leave home. Serve it up as soon as you get there, and then settle in. You'll find it saves on nerves.

The camping budget. Although many people tend to see camping as an economical experience, shopping for food can put an awfully big dent in the budget. Since there are so many little extras that make the trip more enjoyable, why not start purchasing them months before you leave. Keep them on a separate shelf in the basement, and shop from there. It will save you from some of the last-minute crazies, too.

Campstove clean-up. Avoid a lot of time spent cleaning by taking a precaution before cooking. Just as you can line a stove burner at home with aluminum foil, do it with the campstove. In fact, cover as much of it as possible with foil. You'll have less to clean up later.

Camping pots and pans. If you don't have easy clean-up pots and pans for camping, try lining the bottom of the outside of the pan with aluminum foil. It will cut down on the "black" that takes such a long time to clean.

Soap for the outing. Save old pieces of soap

and throw them into a stocking which you tie at both ends. Leave enough stocking to use as "rope". At the campsite, hang the stocking at the faucet. People can clean up quickly without wondering where to put the soap.

Tie up the paper rolls. If your paper towels tend to go rolling during picnic time, put a piece of cord through the center into a loop. If you've got a tree handy, tie it around that and you've got your own paper towel dispenser.

Toilet paper handle. It's always disheartening to find a family member has forgotten to bring back the roll of toilet paper or that it has been dropped along the way. Next time you're camping, string a piece of cord through the roll and tie it into a small loop the size of a pocketbook handle. It's easier to loop it onto your arm, and you don't have to worry about dropping it.

Keeping out the mosquitoes. Try putting nylon netting over your tent as a way to keep out the little buggers. (It'll add a little "safari" flavor to the trip.) Even if you sleep in your car, you can hang the netting over the car so it drapes down on the windows.

Window shades in a can. If you sleep in a station wagon, and it doesn't have curtains, and you'd like a little more privacy, try this. Bring along a can of the foaming window cleaner. Before you go to sleep, foam up the windows on the outside. When you wake up in the morning, just wipe the windows clean. Privacy and clean windows. What could be better than that?

A sweet smelling sleeping bag. Because the bag is so close to the earth, many people complain that their bags retain that damp, muggy smell long after the trip is over. Here are a few things you can do to end that problem. First, after the trip, hang the bag on the line in the sun. There's nothing like fresh air and sunshine to give anything a better scent. And/or add sheets of fabric softener when you store the bag. Or sprinkle baking soda liberally inside. Or get fancy and add a little homemade potpourri (cinnamon sticks will do wonders). You'll have the sweetest smelling sleeping bag the next time you go camping.

A softer sleeping bag. If you'd like just a bit more comfort when you sleep at night, try foam rubber. Buy some 1″ or 1-½″ thick foam, and cut it in pieces to match the length and width of the bags. Because it's so squashable, it doesn't take up that much room.

No more broken eggs. Break the shells before you leave and store the raw eggs in a plastic container that is tightly sealed. When you need eggs, just pour them from the container. No more worry.

Your car can be a washing machine. If it's absolutely necessary to wash clothes on a trip, try this. Bring along a diaper pail. Fill it with dirty clothes, soap and water, and put back the lid. (Make sure it fits tight.) Store it in your trunk. (Do this just before departure to another site or if you're taking a drive.) The movement of the car will agitate your clothes. Just rinse and hang at the next location.

Speedy charcoal fire. Take a large juice can and cut out the top and bottom. Punch holes in the bottom with a can opener all around, about 1" apart. Place in a grill, with the holes being at the bottom of the can. Fill 3/4 full with charcoal. Soak coals with fluid and stuff in a piece of wadded newspaper and add a bit more fluid. Light from the bottom through the holes. In no time you'll have red hot coals. Remove the can with tongs or other protective device and you're ready to grill.

The camping menu. Before you leave on your trip, it's wise to make up a complete menu of what you'll eat at each meal while you're away. Not only will this list help you to shop wisely before you go, but if you post it at the campsite, family will know what's for dinner, and the chef will know what to look for in the supply area.

Baby's crib needs extra protection. For some reason, mosquitoes seem to love the tender young skin of babies. Even if you have protected your tent or car with netting, get some extra nylon netting and place it over baby's crib. You'll have a happier baby in the morning.

Keep a diary. Take notes when you first start camping. Jot down handy tips that you learned from other seasoned campers. Write up meals that were particularly successful. Review the diary before you start organizing for your next trip.

You'll find you get ready faster and the trip is more fun.

Boiling water. If it always seems there is a need for hot or boiling water and your camp has electricity, then bring along a big electric pot. Keep it full of water, always on the boil. You'll have less hassle and more free time.

Shhu food flies. Those annoying flies are never too appetizing, so keep them off your food. Use clear plastic wrap or some of the leftover nylon mosquitoe netting. Both will do the job and because they are see-through, family can locate just the item they want. (If you use the netting, rinse after the meal—it will dry in a flash.)

A soda tote. Save that paperboard soda six-pack tote and bring it on your camping trip. It collapses flat so it takes up no space. When serving meals, fill it with salt, ketchup and other bottles and carry it all to the table at once. Saves steps and makes serving a meal easier.

Serve up some charcoal. If you plan to do a lot of outdoor grilling, you might like to pack individual portions for an evening's meal. This way you don't have to handle a dirty, leaking bag. Throw in just the right amount, and get rid of the bag. Even the kids can help this way.

Packing with baggies. Bring along stackable plastic containers, but whenever possible, pack foods in your cooler in plastic bags. Those that zipper lock are best, but use double twist baggies if you need to. You'll find that you can get almost twice as much in your ice chest when you pack this way. And remember, those things that crush should be packed on top.

Number that meal. If you're like many people who make up salads, hardboiled eggs and other things to eat before you depart, try numbering the cans and containers to match the menu. Containers marked #1 will mean that they go with the first meal of the trip and so forth. This system is an easy one that allows the children to pitch in.

Keep your cooler clean. Finding a milk carton tipped over and spilled can be a lot more annoying on a camping trip than at home. Since little accidents like this seem to be a natural part of camping, cut down on the incidents by wrapping all your "spillables" in zipper lock or twist close plastic bags. If something does spill you'll have almost no clean up. And there is the possibility you'll be able to salvage some of the liquid.

Insulate your sleeping bag. If you love camping, but don't like the cold seeping up through your bag, here are a few tricks to help alleviate that situation. Bring along a piece of carpet remnant and use it as a base for the bag. Or spread a heavy plastic drop cloth (or shower curtain) and use that. If it's quite cold, use a thick layer of newspapers as extra insulation.

OUR FURRY FRIENDS

These days, having pets is becoming more and more commonplace. And while everyone knows the great joy of raising a pet, and the pleasure that you can get from them, you want to be sure that your pet gets the best care possible with the least amount of work and worry for you. Whether your furry friend is a gerbil, a parakeet, a cat, or a dog, we have assembled a group of hints designed to make life with your pet more enjoyable for both of you.

The easy-to-implement hints range from how to keep your gerbil safe while you are cleaning his cage to ways to keep the cat hair off your sofa to an economical tip that will prevent your beloved dog from getting painful rock salt on his paws in snowy season. Of course, we haven't forgotten the fact that sometimes it can be expensive to care for your pet, so we've included tricks that will save you money, too. All of these hints are designed to be simple and direct and will make your pet's life more comfortable, as well as making your life easier, too.

Here's how to handle a new pup that cries all night. In order to get *your* well needed sleep, just wrap an old clock, ticking, in a towel and then put it in the puppy's bed. Another helpful tip is to use a heating pad or a hot water bottle wrapped in a towel; puppies are used to cuddling up to something warm, and they'll even think it's "mom".

Does your grumpy dog refuse to eat? Here's an answer. Perk up your dog's appetite: try some butter and sugar mixed with rice. Pour a bit of beef broth over the mixture and she'll gulp it down! (Of course, check with your dog's vet first to make sure that these foods are all right for your dog's diet, but this formula usually leads to a clean plate!)

Toothless dog? Here's a way to feed her! Usually, when an animal has no teeth, the sight of dog food just turns her off. One good solution is to put all kinds of scraps—meat, vegetables, cheese, etc.—into the blender and puree them. Your dog will gum 'em down in no time.

Hint: Here's a tip to help avoid the usual mess when you open your dog's food can. Simply open both ends of the can with your can opener, then use one lid to push the food through. You'll get the entire can of food out clean as a whistle, no fuss or muss!

Want to keep your dog safe when he goes out at night? Try this to protect your dog from being hit by cars when he takes his nocturnal stroll. Just place a reflecting strip on his collar, and that will alert motorists that he's around. You can also check at your local pet store, for some manufacturers make flea collars that reflect, thus providing two-in-one protection.

Does your pet have trouble when rock salt gets inside his delicate paws? Try this trick. Take 4 small plastic sandwich bags and fasten them to your pet's paws with rubber bands. You'll have instant rainboots!

When you provide plastic "rainboots" for your pet, does he tear through them? This should help. Save a couple of pairs of old socks. Put the socks over the plastic "rainboots" you have created, and your pet will be dry and warm in the worst of weather.

Save your pet in case of fire! Most local fire departments now supply a special sticker which you can place on the windows of the rooms where your pets usually stay. That way, in case of a fire, the firemen will be able to easily identify the room and check it, thus increasing the chance that your pet will be saved.

Here's a good way to assist anyone looking for your pet if he gets lost. Take a good picture of your pet, and list very carefully all of the markings which are on him. Thus, if your pet ever strays, you will have a reliable photo and complete description to supply. This should aid in finding the pet quickly.

Does the can of opened dog food "stink" up your refrigerator? The trick is to store the dog food can inside an empty coffee can with a plastic lid. That'll keep the dog food fresh, and keep the smell clean!

Here's a tip to keep your dog's food from drying up in its plastic bag. Just empty the extra dog food into a jar, large enough to hold the bag of food, then add some vegetable oil and close tightly. The dog food will stay fresh and moist, and your dog will love it.

Here's an easy way to prevent your dog's dishes from sliding all over the kitchen floor! The solution is simple: just place the dog's dishes on a piece of foam rubber! The dishes will "magically" stay in place, and both you and Rover will be happier.

Here's another magic trick. If your dog refuses to take pills, just wrap the pill in some hamburger, cheese, or other good food. Feed this to your dog and "Presto!"—the pill will be down in a flash!

Here's a quick tip to expand your scraps, if you have a fussy dog who turns away his dog food. Simply add some leftover gravy to the dog's dry food, or you can use beef broth made from bouillon cubes. These tricks will give your dog's food a "home-cooked" flavor that will delight him.

Try this way to get a pill down a stubborn dog's throat! First, coat the pill with some butter. Then turn your dog's neck upwards, as if he is looking at the ceiling. Place the pill in his mouth as far back as you possibly can, and then hold his mouth shut, while you rub his neck. He'll swallow automatically!

Here's a great tip to help you tell when your hummingbird feeder is out of water. All you need to do is add red food coloring to the water and you'll be able to tell immediately when the water is low! An extra plus is that hummingbirds are attracted to the red color, and if you paint stripes on the feeder with nail polish, it will also help to attract them.

Here's a novel and decorative way to keep your animals out of the new baby's room without having the door closed! Put a screen door temporarily in place of your regular door!

Does your cat have an injured foot? If the vet tells you to soak your cat's injured foot several times a day, how do you do this without upsetting the cat? Just put the medicine and the water into a small plastic bag. Then, put the cat's foot into the bag and tape it shut. While the foot is soaking, you can hold the cat and pet it so that it feels comfortable, and won't be so frightened.

Here's a way to beat the high cost of pet vitamins. If you give your pet vitamin supplements, try buying them in the drugstore where you buy your own health care products. They are usually priced lower than the vitamins which are specially packaged for animals.

Does your drain get clogged when you bathe your dog in the tub? Here's a simple way to avoid this problem. Take a piece of steel wool and place it over the drain. It will catch the hair before it reaches the drain, and you can simply throw it away when the bath is done!

Is your dog's wire brush full of dog hair? Here's a simple way to get it clean again. Use a toothpick. Just weave the toothpick back and forth through the rows of wire and the hair will magically come loose.

Want to remove that crust that builds up on your aquarium easily? Here's how. First, empty your aquarium. Then scrub it down with nylon net and vinegar. Then rinse it extremely well. The crust will disappear, and when it is clean again, you can replace your fish.

Are you losing your small fish because they are getting sucked up in your bubbleless filter siphon? The solution is to cover the siphon hole with nylon net that has been held in place by a rubber band or string. When you do this, be sure that the tube is not constricted. It'll work like a charm!

Here's how you can make a cheap identification collar for your cat. Take a piece of loosely-fitting elastic and write your name, address, and phone number on it with an indelible pen!

What's the most economical way to keep your cat's litter box fresh? Take some newspapers, shred or tear them, and then mix them with baking soda. The papers will be recycled and they can be easily discarded, and the litter box will smell fresh as a daisy.

Here's a way to make some quick, cheap toys for your cat to play with. Make a ball of nylon net and attach a small bell to the ball your cat will love it! Another good toy can be made by filling a plastic pill bottle with rice, then gluing on the lid.

What can you do if you just can't get up all the cat hairs when you vacuum? Before you vacuum, take a damp broom and sweep over the whole area with it. You'll be happily surprised at the results!

What's the best way to get cat hairs off your chairs? It's easy. Take a damp sponge to them and they'll come right off.

How can you keep your cat from jumping up on tables? When the cat jumps up, spray a little bit of water in its face. This won't hurt your cat in any way, but it won't be long before the cat stops and you'll have broken this bad habit.

Are the plastic plants in your aquarium falling over? Here's a way to keep them upright. Place 3 or 4 marbles on a circle of nylon net, and gather it together. Put the plant stems in the gathered net and fasten the net around the stems with a needle and thread. Then simply place this weighted bag in the gravel, and your plants will be standing straight as can be.

Do your hamster cages rust easily? Here's a trick that can prevent costly replacement. Take a square of tile—any type of household floor or wall tile will do—and place it in the cage. It will do a marvelous job of protecting the cage floor, and cleaning the tile will be easy.

Want an easy way to catch your hamster if he escapes? Make a hole in the lid of a box which is large enough to hold your "escaped" pet. Place a paper towel over this hole and place some enticing morsel of food on the towel. When your hamster is hungry, he'll go for the food, and when he steps on the paper towel, he'll drop into the box below. In order to make sure that he's not hurt, put some crumpled newspaper on the bottom of the box. You'll have him caught in no time!

Does your hamster play on its treadmill and keep you awake with the squeaking? Here's a solution. Use vegetable oil on the treadmill. You can apply it with a cotton swab or ball of cotton. It'll cushion the treadmill, and your hamster will be playing on a sound-proofed surface!

Does your cat keep clawing your good upholstery? It's natural for all cats to "claw", and the cat needs something to claw at. Try nailing a scrap of carpet on a board or box. If you rub catnip on the scratching post, that should help direct your cat to your preferred scratching place, and he'll leave the good furniture alone.

How can you keep ants out of your cat's feeding dish? Take a dish that's larger than the feeding dish. Place a little water in it. Set the feeding dish in this large dish, and that should do the trick!

Want a way to keep your kitten from shedding so much? Some animals just love being vacuumed, and this is one of the best ways to take care of shedding. Start out a little at a time, so that your cat doesn't get scared by the noise of the vacuum, and before you know it, you'll be able to vacuum the entire cat and keep those shedding hairs under control!

How can you keep your dog from tracking mud through the house on those awful rainy days? Just throw old rags or towels at the place where the dog crosses to come into the house. You just can't be there waiting for him every time he comes into the house, but most of the muddy pawprints will be on the towels, not on your waxed floors!

Does your gerbil run away when you clean his cage? Here's how to keep him in one place. Just place your gerbil in the bathtub. Since he can't climb up the sides of the tub, he'll be there until you're finished and ready to put him back into his cage.

Try this tried-and-true way to help your pet if its stomach becomes upset. Just boil some rice and add it to the pet's food. This will act as a binding agent, and will make your animal feel better. Also, you can give your pet some Ka-o-pec-tate, which will serve the same purpose, but be sure to check with your vet before dispensing this tried-and-true medication.

A genuine leather pet collar—for free. The next time one of your leather belts wears out, don't throw it away. Remember that it will make a fine collar for a pet. Cut it down and punch new holes: Fido will be pleased as punch, and very proud.

If your bird makes a mess when he eats and the bird cage doesn't hold all the birdseed, what

can you do? Simple: Just use a large strip of nylon net that's long enough to go around the cage. Wrap it around the cage from the bottom up, allowing about 12 to 15 inches in width, and you'll keep all the seeds INSIDE the cage!

Want a way to stop your bird from pecking at you when you put water in his cage? Simply use a kitchen baster. Fill it with water and then squirt right into the dish!

Here's a quick hint for putting your bird away. Just throw a piece of old sheet over your bird, and then very gently pick him up and put him in the cage. You'll find that this works beautifully, and will keep both *you* and your *bird* happy.

How can you cut the cost of feeding birds outdoors? Easy. Just save your bread crumbs, crust from pizza, etc. and accumulate in a large plastic bowl. Another trick is to empty the bottom of your toaster into the bowl, too. The birds will be thrilled with all these economical crumbs!

Here's a no-cost way to help birds build their nest. Save your strings and dryer lint and when you have a good supply, put it outside for the birds. They will love these materials and use them in nestbuilding.

Perch-cleaning got you down? Here's a quick tip. Take the perch outside and hose it down. Then use an old brush to scrub it. If you happen to have an old suede brush, that would do the job perfectly.

THE KIDS

We all know the joys of having babies and seeing them grow from the infant stage to the creeping and crawling, and toddler times and all the way through the many stages of childhood. And of course, this brings new experiences constantly, which are wonderful. However, the other side of this is the fact that it is a very difficult job to bring up children—and we all need every bit of help that we can get!
So, we have assembled here in this chapter a number of hints that will make your life with your children easier in many ways—from saving steps when your baby cries at night, to keeping children happy and occupied on rainy days, to saving money at birthday time. Each and every hint has been tried and tested on babies and children, and has proved to be a "mother-helper". This chapter will give you help through all the stages of childhood—and we're sure that you will find many of these to be "favorites" that you will use to good advantage. So—if you need help for a baby who is also wriggling around, and threatening to slip in the tub or fall out of a high chair, or ways to keep your school-age children amused and teach them some reading or math at the same time—you'll find a way to do it all right here!

Do your baby's bottles keep that "sour" smell from all the milk? Even if they are clean, it's easy to have that happen. Here's a tip that'll rid you, and your baby, of that awful odor. Just soak the bottle overnight in a heavy solution of baking soda and water.

Here's another great use for baking soda. Although many "regular" fabric softeners can chafe or irritate your little one, ordinary baking soda will not. Just add it to the wash cycle.

A little food coloring in the bath will make bathing a treat. Just a couple of drops and your kids will clamor for the tub. A quick rinse, and the color is gone.

Remember this simple tip: a child in colorful clothes is easier to find. Nothing stands out in a crowd like a toddler in red, purple or yellow.

Old, cleaned, detergent bottles may be great toys. For summer fun, your kids will love this cheap, quick "squirt gun" you've invented for them.

Here's a little tip to get some extra mileage out of sleepwear. When your baby outgrows his sleepers, just cut the feet off them, and he'll be able to use them a lot longer.

Does your baby spit up during a bath? Here's a way to prevent that. Sometimes babies can throw up if they're bathed immediately after being fed. Try bathing the baby before a feeding—that should cut down the problem considerably.

Here's an inexpensive and easy way to bathe baby when he's outgrown his infant tub.

Buy the largest and softest woven plastic laundry basket you can find. Place it in the tub, fill the tub with water, and bathe your baby. The water can flow in and out, and you've got enough room to bathe baby.

Warm up your baby's crib on cool winter nights. Most parents don't remember how cold those plastic crib liners can get. To avoid this problem, simply take a large beach towel and place it over the plastic liner. Then put on the crib sheet. Baby will sleep nice and warm all night through and the mattress will still be protected.

Here's a tip that'll make your child's wagon last a lot longer! Drill a few small holes in the bottom. That way, the water will drain out after a rainstorm and the wagon won't rust!

Want a way to outsmart the baby that shakes his crib and walks it across the room? The way to solve this problem is to place "bunion pads" under each leg of the crib. Then, when the baby tries to walk that crib, it won't crawl!

This is a surefire way to improvise a seat for your child when visiting. It's really easy—just use a few books or even a couple of phone books. This can be coupled with using a small pillow as a softener.

This is a simple trick to keep spills from making your baby's high chair tray a mess! Just put it in the yard, turn on your lawn hose, and let that do the job for you!

Does your baby keep sliding down in his

high chair? This can help you stop that uncomfortable situation. Take an old towel or blanket and fasten it to the back of the high chair. Baby will stay nice and still.

Does your baby fall out of his high chair easily? Here's a way to prevent this dangerous accident. Place the high chair against a wall. Then attach a large hook to the back of the chair, and the "eye" in the wall. Just hook the chair to the wall, and your baby will be safe and sound, and will not be able to overturn the chair.

Try this simple way to prevent your baby from falling out of the high chair. Take an old blanket, cut it in half, and roll the two pieces. Then place them on either sides of the baby. This will make the high chair seat tight, so baby won't be likely to fall.

If you've discovered that your toddler is allergic to the stuffing in toys, here's a way to save a beloved stuffed animal. Remove all of the stuffing from the toy and replace it with old panty hose or non-allergic filling. You'll be able to wash the stuffed toy as often as you need to, and your child will be able to have a favorite toy.

Would your baby like some entertainment during bath time? A bath can sometimes be a scary event for a baby. So make bathtime a happier event with this trick. Hang a mobile above the sink so your baby can look up and amuse himself, rather than just being able to stare at a blank wall.

Here's a way to keep the baby's bottle supplies together in your dishwasher. Place all your baby's supplies in a nylon net bag that closes with a drawstring, or even stockings. That way, all of the supplies will stay together and not "wander" all over the dishwasher.

No more missing socks! When you buy socks, buy them all in the same color. Then, if you happen to lose a sock in the laundry, you'll be able to continue mating the remaining socks. This trick works well for the whole family.

Do your baby bottles leak when you travel? Here's a way to keep those plastic bottles leak-free. Take a piece of plastic wrap or aluminum foil and put it over the bottle opening, then add nipple and cap. This should keep the bottle tight so that you will avoid leaks.

Is your little girl reluctant to give up her dolls? Try this. Instead of taking them away, display them on bookshelves or hang them from the ceiling. That way she won't feel so deprived of her "friends".

Here's a good way to keep your baby's bottle warm when you go outdoors. After the baby's bottle is warmed to the correct temperature, just pop it into a wide mouth thermos that has been "warmed" with hot water. Put on the lid. This will keep the bottle just right, so that when your baby is hungry, the bottle will be ready.

Try this novel game at your child's next party. Ask each of your child's guests to bring along an old photo. Then put the pictures on the wall. Whoever guesses the most names correctly, wins! It's a great way to break the ice.

Want a good way to wean your baby from his bottle? When the time comes to start weaning your baby from the bottle, take the lid off the bottle and let the baby drink from the "old favorite" bottle, then start using a cup from there. Make sure you start with baby's favorite drinks. This is a good transition that makes the weaning process so much easier.

Candle craft for the kids. If you really want to bring joy to the kids, help them to make their own candles. Caution: Be sure to be there to supervise. Simply melt down stubs in an old can which you've set over very low heat. Find a mold—another old can or milk carton will do—and presto, you've got new candles. Be sure to include a wick.

Here's a good way to make sure you never run out of pre-moistened towelettes for your baby. All you need is two ingredients—a supply of diaper liners which can be used as wipes, and a thermos of warm water, which can be used to wet the liners. It's easy and inexpensive, and you'll have a good supply handy at all times.

Here's an easy way to dry out a damp bed so your baby can go back into a pleasant, dry crib. Take your portable hair dryer and use it to quickly dry out the spots which are damp. Not only will the baby go back into a nice dry bed, but it will be pleasantly warm as well. You can even scent the mattress to make it smell extra fresh.

This is a good way to keep your baby from tearing off a bandage on his hand or foot. Take a sock or stocking and slip it over the bandaged hand or foot.

Does your baby fuss when you try to cut his nails? Here's a sure-fire trick. Wait until baby is napping or asleep to cut his nails.

Here's a way to stop the "dropped pacifier" trick. Take a piece of colorful string and attach it to the pacifier. Then pin the string to the baby's clothing. The pacifier will stay off the ground, and the problem will be eliminated.

This is a good way to clean a mesh playpen. Take a solution of detergent and water, with some bleach added. Place it in an old spray bottle. Spray, soaking the solution into the mesh. Use an old brush to do a thorough job. Be sure to rinse 3 times in order to eliminate the detergent, in case your child likes to chew on his playpen.

Does your toddler always walk around with a favorite blanket until it's in shreds? Cut the blanket in quarters. That way, when one quarter is beyond use, you'll have three in reserve to keep his favorite "blankie" going longer.

Here's a great step-saver. When a child is sick, he often needs you, if only for support and love. One way to keep from running back and forth, checking on him is to give your child a bell. That way, he can ring it, and you'll be there in no time.

This is a simple way to make sure that your baby doesn't have to have a cold diaper when you change him at night. Keep a heating pad set on low with the diapers. It will keep the top two toasty, so that when your baby is ready to be changed, you'll have the diapers warmed up and ready.

Baby got gum in her hair? It may take a little courage to try this the *first* time, but see how well it works. The next time one of the children shows up with a big was of gum in the hair, use freshly chewed gum to get it out. Push it down onto the gum you want dislodged. The old gum will stick to the new.

The many uses of a laundry basket. . . Use a sturdy plastic laundry basket (solid, without open weaving is best). It can be placed out of sight, and has no hard corners that are dangerous.

Here's a good way to improvise a dressing table for your baby. Take a card table which is very sturdy and cover it with a mattress pad cut to fit. This makes an absolutely perfect dressing table at very little cost, and the table can go on to serve many purposes later on.

Make an instant bowling alley. Partially fill some used detergent bottles with dirt so that you weight the bottoms down. Set them up in your driveway, or down in the basement. Supply a rubber ball, and presto!

Is there life after coloring books? Here's

one for a dismal day. Use up your old newspapers. Just give them to your kids, and tell them to express themselves. They can cut out words, sentences, or funny pictures and then glue them down to other funny pictures! You'll even wonder if they've slipped out, they'll be so engrossed.

Another recipe which will make some inexpensive "play dough". Mix 3 cups of flour with 1 cup of salt. Slowly add 2 cups of hot water and mix well. Knead the dough for 15 minutes (get the kids to help), and store in a cool place.

Have you ever lost your child in a crowd? If so, try this. Tie a whistle around his or her neck, and tell them to blow it repeatedly if they lose you.

Use this economical way to store your child's small collectibles. When you use those large coffee cans, save them. Smooth over any jagged edges. Then paint and glue the cans together. Then you can either place them on their sides so you have a bunch of cubbyholes or you can cap them with the plastic top and use them individually.

Turn that old calendar over to the kids. Let them cut out all the pretty pictures and use them in their next picture-making project. Or cut up the numbers and use them too. What might look like junk to you is often pretty intriguing to a child.

Make your kids' money hard-to-lose when they go swimming. If your child is always losing money when he goes to the swimming pool, try this. Sew a small pocket onto an old towel. You'll fasten it shut with a safety pin, and the money will be safe "locked" inside.

Lunchbag for the kids. You know how little girls love to dress up in mommy's clothes. Well, here's a technique to make sure lunch is not forgotten. Turn that old worn-out handbag of yours into a lunch tote. It's guaranteed to increase the "remembrance factor" when kids take lunch to school.

Try this trick to encourage your baby to drink from a cup! Fill your baby's bottle with some liquid that isn't a favorite, maybe some diluted milk, and put the liquid he likes best in the cup. When the times comes to taste both, there's an excellent chance that he'll pick the one in the cup!

Stop those arguments about which TV programs to watch! Allow the children to vote on the programs. They'll learn to take turns, as each child gets to watch his or her favorite, and learn how democracy works, too.

Try this safe version of "pin the tail on the donkey". If you're worried that the perennial favorite game of Pin the Tail on the Donkey is too dangerous, try this substitute. Draw a big bunny rabbit and instead of pins, stick scotch tape on some cotton balls and use them to "pin the Bunny Tail". Put a color dot on the ball as I.D. It's just as much fun and you won't worry about pricked fingers.

Try this trick to organize your children when they leave for school in the morning. Place a box or plastic basket in your child's room. Each night, put all the school things in the basket—homework, reports, mittens, boots, money, books, etc. The next morning, your child is ready to go.

Does your baby's bottle slip when he holds it? Here's a way to keep it steady. Take a small sock and make it into a tube or a stocking. Then simply slip the baby's bottle inside, and baby will be able to hold it nice and steady.

Here's a way to cut down on dressing time for the kids. If your little girl has certain "outfits", save time by hanging them together as a group. If there are socks, too, just pin them to the dress with a safety pin.

Here's a safe and easy way to prevent your baby from slipping during a bath. When you bathe your baby, keep him dressed in a T-shirt. That way, you can hold him easily, and he won't slip and slide around in the tub.

Do your baby bottle nipples get clogged, no matter how much you clean them? Here's a simple trick that will take care of this problem. Take a toothpick or a large needle and gently push it through the nipple hole. It will clear the nipple very easily.

Try this on poor, old teddy! Cut a small opening in the bottom of the damaged toy. Remove all of the stuffing and hand wash the "animal" in cold water. Be sure to remove any trim that might be damaged or might "run" in the wash. Blow dry the toy, or use the regular laundry dryer if the toy is large. Then restuff with a washable filler, such as foam or cut-up panty hose. Stitch the opening closed and you'll have a toy that's good as new!

Try this recipe for some "play clay". Heat 2-1/2 cups of salt and 1 cup of water until just boiling. Then mix 1-1/2 cups of cornstarch with 3/4 cup of water. Add this to the salt and water mixture. Stir until it is thick. If necessary, add more water or cornstarch for consistency. Stir until it is thick. Cool and store in the refrigerator.

If you're short on closet space, here's a way to hang your baby's clothes. Take a round shower curtain hoop, suspend it from the ceiling, and make sure it's secure. Then take baby's clothes and hang them from the hoop. You'll have instant extra closet space that's colorful and decorative, too.

Does your child slip down in his stroller? Here's a hint to alleviate that. Seat your baby in a small seat, like a feeder chair. Then place the seat inside your stroller. That way, he'll sit safely, and you'll still be able to wheel him easily.

Here's a good way to keep your toddler from slipping through the rail of a bunk bed when visiting. Take a bed sheet or old blanket. Hang it over the bunk bed rail. Tuck it under the mattress. This will form a protective "netting" that will help to keep your child safe and sound. If you use 2 layers, that will make the protection even better.

Here's an inexpensive way to help your child "redecorate". Try this for a new headboard, which will give a new "look" to her room. Use the old headboard as a base, and tack some fabric over it.

Try this easy hint for preventing your small child from bumping into his bed. If your child is getting bruised from hitting his legs on the corner of the bed, try tying some layers of fabric on the legs of the bed. If you have some spare rubber foam, this will give added cushioning.

Here's a way to give your baby his late-night feeding without having to make an extra trip to the kitchen. Heat the baby's bottle to the correct temperature before you go to bed. Fill a wide mouth thermos bottle with very hot water so that it becomes warm. Then pour out the hot water, and place the baby bottle inside. Close the lid. All you need do is keep this next to the baby's crib and when feeding times comes, it will be waiting there for you—at just the right temperature!

Save those game boards from looking "ratty". Before you give any game boards to your children, coat them with some clear shellac. This protective coating will do wonders to lengthen the life of the boards!

Here's a really novel way to make an exciting birthday cake. Instead of using a regular pan, try using ice-cream cones! Fill the cones half full with cake batter, bake in muffin tins and presto! You've got something completely different! Ice after they cool, and your little guests will beg for seconds.

Here's a neat and "crafty" way to organize a child's room even when you can't afford a storage area for sports equipment. Take a large carton and have the kids decorate it with "graffiti". Then place all of your child's baseball bats, footballs, hockey sticks, etc. in the carton.

Why be bored? Build your own miniature golf course! Here's all you do. Just set aside some space in your backyard, or in a nearby vacant lot, as long as you check with the owner to make sure it's OK. Just "plot" out your own course, using some old tin cans or plastic bottles cut in tow, or even dixie cups, placed in the ground as holes! It's cheap, fun, and it'll make you the envy of your neighborhood!

Save your child's old clothing. Dirty activities deserve old worn-out clothes. Let them get as dirty as they want, then throw out the clothes. This will seem like a special treat.

Here's a tip to make it easier for a baby to use a spoon. Instead of always using household metal spoons, which are cold and hard, try a small plastic spoon, similar to the type that comes with ice cream. Then just toss them out at the end of every meal.

Are your child's stuffed animals grimy and

dingy? If the animals are stuffed with an unwashable filler, sprinkle some cornmeal or cornstarch on them to clean them. Let it set, and then brush it, and the dirt, out!

Do the plastic bottles your baby uses have an unpleasant odor? Here's a way to deal with this problem. Boil the bottles for 3 minutes in a solution of 3 tablespoons baking soda and water. The odor will miraculously disappear.

Are you nervous about visiting because your child may wet the bed? Here's an old trick that will make visitng a pleasure. Take an old plastic tablecloth on all of your travels and just slip it over the mattress. That way, your host's mattress will be protected, and you'll all sleep easier.

If you have a child who keeps asking for something to drink all night long, here's a way to keep him happy. Keep a bottle of water or a favorite drink that won't spoil on your child's night table. That way, when he cries for a drink you won't have to run into the kitchen, and if your child is old enough, he can pour for himself without disturbing you at all.

Here's a way to keep a parent present even if he or she has to do a great deal of travelling. Have the parent read some favorite stories or entertaining jokes onto a tape. Then, when the time is appropriate, just turn on the tape and "daddy" or "mommy" will be right there. This makes the absence a little bit easier on everyone.

Are you nervous about small children getting into your car and possibly smashing their fingers in the car door? Try this for some relief. Before closing the car door, say something like "OK, everyone, clap your hands! Now, do it again!" This will reassure you that precious fingers are safe, and small children will feel that you're playing a fun game, so it will keep them entertained, too.

Want an inexpensive way to stretch your baby powder? Mix the baby powder with a box of cornstarch or some baking soda and it will go much further. Both of these materials are safe and will stretch your money, too. Cornstarch is just fine to use alone.

A formula for shoelaces? You bet. Count the total number of holes on each side of your child's shoes, then multiply that number by 3. That's the number of inches to buy. So, for example, if there are 12 holes, multiply 12 by 3 and you'll get 36, which means you should buy 36 inch laces.

Does your baby's bottle get mixed up with other bottles when you visit? Initial the bottles with red nail polish or a strip of electrician's tape. That way, you'll be able to easily identify which bottle belongs to *your* baby.

Want a quick way to let your child's friends know which apartment is yours when they get off the elevator? Hang a stuffed toy on your front door. It will be easily spotted, and it will be more fun to visit.

A space-saving way to play musical chairs. If your space is tight, but your guests just love to play musical chairs, try using magazines for the children to stand on instead of chairs. Cleaning up after is faster without a lot of chairs to put away.

Here's a cheap and easy way to make "dolls"! Save used, clean, empty dishwashing detergent bottles. Take some colored marking pens and draw faces, hair, and clothes on them. Before long, you'll have a whole "family" of these beautiful friends.

Does your child always spill drinks? Switch to heavier weighted glasses or even a small mug.

Save your greeting cards for the kids. They're perfect to cut out for drawings, they can use a bunch of them to make a montage. Or best yet, keep some stickers handy to paste down over the old signature and let your children "decorate" a new card.

Help your baby to sleep better when a cold or the flu sets in. Simply prop up the head of your baby's bed using spare pillows under the crib mattress. In this elevated position, baby will be able to breathe more easily.

Here's a way to keep baby bottles from falling over when you store them in the refrigerator. Take a cardboard carton used for soft drinks, that has segmented compartments. The compartments should hold six bottles, and this device will keep your baby bottles upright. Also, a six-pack of bottles is easy to carry with you.

Keep your child's shoes looking good as new. First, shine them well before wearing. Then, as scuffs appear, take a colored felt-tip pen and use it to cover up the scuffs and scratches. Vaseline also helps to protect the leather.

Dry your baby quick 'n easy. Instead of a bath towel, use the oversized bath towels or a huge beach towel to dry your baby. These big towels give you plenty of drying surface and it's easier to hold your baby secure.

Try this idea for a child's "instant desk". Find a large, sturdy cardboard box. Cut off the flaps and cut it down if necessary. Then cut out a semi-circle from the bottom of one side of this box. The cut-out circle will form a hole for your child's legs. The bottom of the box will serve as the desk top. Let your child decorate the sides with personalized pictures.

Want a fast way to get the chalky deposit out of your baby's bottles? Vinegar is a miracle household item, capable of handling so may tasks (besides a great salad). Boil bottles in a solution of water with 2-½ cups of vinegar for 15 minutes. This should cut that chalky deposit. As a general rule, if you have hard water, always throw in a little vinegar to prevent the build-up to begin with. Your baby will have sparkling clean bottles all the time.

Think ahead! People get their feelings hurt easily. If you invite children to a party who wear braces, consider them when planning your menu. Be sure to have foods they can eat, too. Apples, rock candy, anything that might harm their tender gums or their braces should be eliminated. After all, we can resist anything except temptation.

Give your child some help in pulling the difficult zipper on his coat. Little hands have trouble grasping those zipper pulls, so make bigger ones. Take a novelty chain, a shower curtain hook, even a jumbo paper clip, and attach it to the zipper pull. That way, there will be something big for your child to grab onto.

Try this easy way to keep your toddler's plastic toys neat after he plays with them in the bath tub. Hang a 5 or 10 lb. size, nylon potato bag over the faucet handle, filled with the soppy toys that your toddler has played with at bath time. They'll be all together, and able to dry easily, and you'll eliminate the mess.

Recycle those toys to keep your kid interested! If your child tires of toys easily, try rotating them! Pack a group of toys up for a few weeks (or even months), and then when you bring them out again, it'll seem like Christmas!

Has your toddler ever managed to get locked in the bathroom? This upsetting experience has hit most families. There's a simple solution to prevent the problem. Take an old mattress cover or blanket and place it over the top of the bathroom door. Your child will be able to close the bathroom door partially, giving privacy, but not completely, so there will be no danger of getting locked in.

Do you have an adventurous child who always pulls drawers out? This simple solution will prevent bruises. Take an old stocking and wedge it into the side of the drawer. Small toddlers will find it hard to remove the stocking, and so the drawer will remain in place.

This is a good way to teach your child how to put on a coat. Place the coat on the floor, with the lining facing up. Then have your child at the top end of the coat, bend over and slip his arms into the sleeves of the coat. Then just toss the coat over his head, and the coat will be in place.

This is a way to dress your child and keep him amused at the same time. Try dressing in front of a mirror or put a screen with colorful decals in front of your child. You will furnish entertaining distraction during dressing time.

Try this simple way to make a barrette hold in thin hair. In order to get the barrette to grip well on your little girl's hair, take a small strip of rubber foam and glue it on the inside of the barette. It will work wonders.

Make sure your child can reach his clothes. To develop independence, a child needs to be able to reach his or her own clothes, Never store every-day wearables above their reach.

Kids always running in and out of your house? Perhaps they are just checking the time. Try putting a clock facing out of a window and letting them know where to look.

Has your child outgrown his favorite sweater? Don't throw it away. Chances are, it's only the sleeves that are too short. Cut off the sleeves and finish the armholes, and he'll have a great sweater vest to wear.

An old plastic clothes basket makes a great toy box. Sit the basket outside the back door. Tell your children to deposit their outdoor toys in the basket as they come inside, and they'll always know where their toys are.

Is your child a messy eater? Try putting his tuna salad, or egg salad sandwich in an ice-cream cone.

Is your baby's high chair a mess? A few minutes in the shower will take care of that and save you a lot of scrubbing.

Rainy day fun for the kids, and math practice, too! Take an old egg carton and let your kids toss pennies, nickels and dimes into the egg cups. They can add up the total number of coins that they land in the cups, after each turn, and check the totals with you, the judge. The winners can get a prize—and they'll be practicing their math, too!

Try this inexpensive way to provide children's party treats. Save the empty rolls from your bathroom tissue or the rolls from wax paper, aluminum foil, etc. Fill the empty rolls with candy. Then wrap in tissue paper and tie both ends of the roll with yarn. You'll have a decorative party favor that is inexpensive and extra fun to open.

When traveling with your baby, remember this. Give your baby his or her bottle when landing *and* taking off, to reduce air pressure. For the older kids, have plenty of chewing gum.

If you want your kids to sleep while traveling, remember this. Most colas have as much caffeine as coffee. Don't expect the tykes to nap if you've just given them a soft drink.

Does baby unroll the toilet paper? Before putting it on the roll, shape it into a square, and it won't turn quite so easily.

If baby is fussy and won't eat fruit or veggies, here's a helpful hint. Puree them in a blender. The kid will love them.

Quick tips:

- A drop of iodine on a splinter will make it show up easier.
- A damp wash-cloth stored in a plastic bag will come in very handy on trips with your kids.
- Add a little dishwashing detergent to your child's water-colors, and spills will mop up easier.
- Tie your baby's favorite rattle to his or her wrist with a length of colored yarn.
- Eye-drops will go in easier if the child is lying down on his or her back.

- Old bedspreads make great "tents" on rainy days.
- Always "reward" your child for doing the right thing, even if it's just with a smile.